MIKE BURNS
774 263 8000

SUNBEAM ALPINE
AND TIGER

Other Titles in the Crowood AutoClassics Series

SUNBEAM ALPINE AND TIGER
The Complete Story

Graham Robson

The Crowood Press

First published in 1996 by
The Crowood Press Ltd
Ramsbury, Marlborough
Wiltshire SN8 2HR

www.crowood.com

Paperback edition 2003

British Library Cataloguing-in-Publication Data
A catalogue record for this book is available from the British Library.

ISBN 1 86126 636 7

Picture Credits
All photographs courtesy of Mirco Decet, Barry Littlewood and Steve Bagley from the Museum of British Road Transport, and the author.

Printed and bound in Great Britain by The Bath Press

Contents

Acknowledgements

You could say that I started preparing this book in 1957 – but that was years before I even started working as a writer. Even so, as many people made this book possible from those days as did those who helped me more recently.

From my days in and around Coventry, I am grateful to Norman and Lewis Garrad for first hiring me into the Rootes 'works' rally team, for that is where I first came close to the Rapiers and Alpines of the period. For similar reasons, I need to thank my good friend Harry Webster who, as technical director of Standard-Triumph, let me take time off work to go rallying for a rival organization!

Maurice Smith of *Autocar,* now no longer with us, not only installed me into the Coventry office of that magazine at the right time, where I could meet various Rootes personalities *and* the cars which are the stars of this book, but also let me play with his own Tigers from time to time.

Marcus Chambers and his assistant Ian Hall, who took over from the Garrad-controlled operation in the Rootes competition department, helped me then, and helped me a lot more recently, for both retain vivid memories of the competition exploits of the period.

From my own Rootes days, which immediately followed the Alpine/Tiger period,

I'm happy to salute Roy Axe, Peter Wilson, Mike Jones and Don Tarbun, plus Kevin Beattie of Jensen Motors in West Bromwich. Roy was the young designer/stylist who came to head the Rootes design studios, while Peter Wilson was the development chief who usually managed to insert some character into the mundane new cars which his elders (but not betters) wanted to put on sale.

Mike and Don not only had close connections with the Alpine and Tiger, but later came to work with me during my years at Rootes/Chrysler. I came to know Kevin Beattie well during the 'Tiger period' at Jensen, but it was typical of the gentleman that he was, that secrets were never divulged.

More recently, in preparing the book, Mirco Decet not only provided all the new photography, but found and captured the cars we needed to illustrate in colour. Barry Littlewood and Steve Bagley (from the Museum of British Road Transport in Coventry) allowed me to browse through their extensive Rootes archives, and provided many of the black-and-white pictures.

Last, and not least, I want to thank every Sunbeam enthusiast for making this story worth writing, and especially the Sunbeam Talbot Alpine Register for helping to keep the cars alive.

Introduction

My interest in Alpines was sparked by the rumours which were circulating in Coventry when I started working there at the end of 1957. The more I heard, the more I got enthralled. You could say that I've been fascinated by Alpines ever since. I lived there throughout the 1960s, long enough to see the car's entire career blossom, then die away.

Not that I believed all those rumours at first. Rootes was developing a sports car. Rootes? A sports car? Don't be ridiculous, I thought – Rootes has never been in the sports car business. Then, later, I heard that Armstrong-Siddeley was to build a sports car. Armstrong-Siddeley? A sports car? I'd seen the sort of cars Armstrong-Siddeley liked to build, so it was even more ridiculous...

Perhaps this explains why so many car nuts like me always found the Rootes Alpines, and the Tigers which followed them, to be such interesting machines. During the fourteen years when I lived and worked close to Coventry I must have driven, or been driven in, dozens of Rootesmobiles, then went to work in the Rootes Engineering Division for a time, so I reckon I now know as much about Rootes, its thinking, and its heritage, as the next man.

I never owned an Alpine, or a Tiger, when they were new cars – marriage, young children and dogs had a lot to do with that – but as a privileged young motoring writer it was surprising how often one or other of the cars was parked in my driveway.

Then, and later, I always thought that these cars never got their share of sports car publicity. MGs were everywhere, Triumphs were successful, and Austin-Healeys were the glamorous race and rally winners. In spite of their great performance at Le Mans, though, the Alpines seemed to be neglected.

One day, I knew, I would like to write a book about the cars – a book not submerged in sentiment, and a book which got its heritage right. I wanted to explain how the Alpine developed, where it came from, and who were the personalities behind its career. I wanted to double-check the Husky and Rapier connections, the vital dates which governed when and how the Alpine was born, and died, and why the Alpine was built, marketed and sold in the way which became so familiar.

Even though Chrysler dumped most of the records when it took over at Rootes, and even though many important personalities have left us, I hope I have got it right.

If you are someone who likes his sports car motoring without leaks, without draughts, and without silly temperament, an Alpine of the 1960s might be for you. On the other hand, if you are someone who likes his horsepower in big V8 dollops, his tyres habitually scrabbling for grip, and his ears filled with the unmistakeable wuffle of an eight-cylinder exhaust, you might consider a Tiger.

And even if you're not, you ought to read this book to find out what you are missing!

Alpine and Tiger Evolution

Date	Event
October 1954	The very first version of a new family of ohv four-cylinder engines was announced. At first used only in the existing (old-style) Minx Mk VIII, this was then a 43bhp/1,390cc unit, with a three-main-bearing crankshaft.
October 1955	The first Sunbeam Rapier – the very first of an entirely new family of Rootes family cars – was announced. This car would eventually be the donor vehicle for a (shortened) floorpan and the major chassis/running gear components for the future Alpine.
1956/7	Work on a new Rootes Group sports car began in the Styling Department at Humber Road, Coventry, using the new-generation Hillman Husky floorpan as a basis.
January 1958	The Rapier/Minx based Hillman Husky Series I, which would donate its short-wheelbase floorpan to the Sunbeam Alpine, was announced.
1958	Prototype development of Rootes sports cars began in secret, much work being done by Armstrong-Siddeley at Parkside, Coventry. Though not yet revealed, Rootes had decided that Armstrong-Siddeley should manufacture the new sports car, now titled Alpine.
July 1959	The new Alpine sports car (retrospectively known as Alpine I) was announced, with 78bhp/1,494cc engine. Manufacture and final assembly was centred at the Armstrong-Siddeley works.
October 1960	The Alpine SII took over from Alpine I, with 80bhp/1,592cc engine.
March 1961	The Sussex-based coachbuilders, Thomas Harrington Ltd, announced much modified versions of the Alpine, called Harrington-Alpines. Backed, but not manufactured, by the Rootes Group, these cars were in production for two years, their body shapes eventually being used by the 'works' team for racing at Le Mans.
June 1961	Two 'works' Alpines competed in the Le Mans 24 Hour race, one of them finishing sixteenth (driven by Peter Harper/Peter Procter), and winning the Index of Thermal Efficiency.

September 1961	Ford-USA introduced an entirely new type of 'small' ohv V8 engine. This would eventually be taken up for the Sunbeam Tiger project in 1964.
March 1962	End of assembly of Alpines at the Armstrong-Siddeley factory. Almost simultaneously, assembly of Alpines began at the main Rootes factory at Ryton-on-Dunsmore, Coventry.
March 1963	Introduction of the Alpine III to replace the Alpine II, including a new style hardtop option/much modified interior. Two versions were available – a Tourer with 82bhp/1,592cc, or a GT with 78bhp/1,592cc.
March 1963	Carroll Shelby's company (already famous for inspiring and producing the AC Cobra) was contracted to produce prototypes of a Ford V8-engined car, originally called the 'Thunderbolt'. This was the birth of the Tiger project.
January 1964	The Alpine III replaced by Alpine IV, this time only with the 82bhp engine tune, with an automatic transmission option, and with re-styled body including deletion of fins.
April 1964	New Ford V8-engined Tiger introduced, with 136bhp/4,261cc engine. Originally only for sale in North America. All Tigers were assembled at Jensen of West Bromwich, in the West Midlands.
June 1964	Rootes announced a financial deal with Chrysler-USA. Chrysler immediately took a 30 per cent voting share and a 50 per cent non-voting share of Rootes's capital.
October 1964	New corporate all-synchromesh gearbox fitted to all medium-sized Rootes cars, including Alpine sports car.
March 1965	Tiger went on sale in the UK in RHD form.
September 1965	Series V Alpine took over from Series IV, this time with an enlarged, 92.5bhp/1,725cc engine. This was the first and only derivative of this type to have a five-main-bearing crankshaft.
January 1967	The Tiger II (with 174bhp/4,727cc) officially took over from the Tiger I, though Tiger IIs were officially only sold in the USA.
January 1967	With British government approval, Chrysler-USA officially took a majority financial stake in Rootes.
June 1967	The last Tiger of all was produced by Jensen.
January 1968	The last Alpine V of all was produced, at Ryton-on-Dunsmore.

1 The Rootes Group and its Sunbeam-Talbots

The story of the Alpines and Tigers of the 1960s starts many years before Ken Howes and Geoff Crompton began to shape a clay model at Humber Road in Coventry. It starts well before the family of ohv engines which powered the Alpines were even conceived. It starts, in fact, with the first Lord Rootes, his highly developed ego, and his North American ambitions.

To long-time Rootes-watchers like myself, the miracle was that Rootes ever managed to make such a car, for in the 1940s and 1950s there had been precious little sporting character in new Rootes models – lots of sporting heritage, which the Rootes family had wasted after they had bought it up, but no character.

This story, then, begins in the 1930s, when the Rootes Group was formed, and when two tottering independent marques – Sunbeam and Talbot – were swept up by an ambitious Billy Rootes. Starting from nothing in the 1920s, by the end of the 1930s Rootes had become Great Britain's fourth largest car makers, with 11 per cent of the market.

Having already become Britain's largest (and probably most profitable) motor traders – though Rootes rarely admitted to such, Billy Rootes and his younger brother Reginald first took a stake in Standard, but discarded it, then considered buying up Clyno of Wolverhampton, and abandoned that too. Finally, with financial aid from the Prudential Assurance Company, they

Billy Rootes (later Lord Rootes – right), and his brother Sir Reginald ruled their Group with an iron hand from the 1920s to 1964, when Chrysler stepped in.

injected capital into Humber and Hillman, encouraged them to merge, and eventually emerged as majority shareholders.

The Rootes Group, as an official business, came into existence in 1932, with Humber Ltd. as its wholly owned manufacturing subsidiary. Its next move was to buy up the Sunbeam and Talbot businesses in 1935, both of which companies were part of the collapsing Sunbeam-Talbot-Darracq combine, which had defaulted on long-term loan repayments and had been speedily split up by its bankers.

Amazingly, when Rootes rescued the two

11

Rootes: the dynasty

During his working life at Rootes, William ('Billy') became Sir William, then Lord Rootes. He was the engine, the inspiration, the dictator, in fact the outright ruler of his empire – and without his approval the Alpine would never have reached the showrooms.

William Rootes (senior) was the owner of a cycle shop in Hawkhurst, in Kent, who fathered two sons, William (born in 1894) and Reginald (born in 1896). While the sons were at school, the father expanded to become a motor trader, by 1914 being ready to sell a multitude of different makes and models.

Neither son showed much interest in the family business at first, William becoming a pupil at Singer Motors in Coventry, Reginald training to be an accountant and working at the Admiralty. Immediately after the First World War, however, the brothers got together, developing Rootes Ltd in Maidstone, then expanding this business to become Britain's largest mid-1920s motor car distributors, based in Devonshire House in London's famous Piccadilly, opposite the Ritz hotel.

After buying Thrupp & Maberly (a London coachbuilder), with backing from the cash rich Prudential Assurance Co., Rootes then moved on to take stakes in two Coventry based car-makers, Hillman and Humber. Complex behind-the-scenes moves then saw Hillman and Humber merge, and Rootes take control, thus founding the Rootes Group.

By 1935 Rootes had not only rationalized the business, introducing totally new Hillman and Humber ranges, but it had also purchased Sunbeam and Talbot from the Receiver (see the panel on page 14). From this point the Rootes Group had a market share of more than 10 per cent, and was now the fourth-ranking of Britain's 'Big Six' car makers.

The next two decades were frenetic. In the late 1930s Rootes set up Sunbeam-Talbot, built and ran enormous Government 'shadow' factories at Ryton-on-Dunsmore (near Coventry), and Speke (near Liverpool). In the late 1940s it concentrated all its car assembly resources on Ryton, then took over Singer in the winter of 1955/1956, completing a quintet of marques. Along the way 'Billy' Rootes became the first Lord Rootes in 1959, and his son Geoffrey became increasingly influential in running the manufacturing side.

Long after the Alpine sports car was established, Rootes was persuaded to build a new factory at Linwood, near Glasgow airport, where the rear-engined Imp was built from 1963. Unhappily, a thirteen week strike at a body-making subsidiary in 1961, which affected the entire group, and heavy investment in the Linwood plant, brought Rootes into financial crisis, and a rescue from outside became essential.

Chrysler of Detroit took a financial stake in 1964, by which time Lord Rootes was mortally ill. After he died, in December 1964, his brother Sir Reginald became chairman, and Geoffrey inherited the Barony. Chrysler then went on to take a majority stake (67 per cent) in 1967, mopping up minority holdings in the next few years. This was the point at which Lord (Geoffrey) Rootes became chairman of the Group.

Rootes was renamed Chrysler United Kingdom Ltd in 1970, after which all remaining traces of Rootes ownership were speedily expunged.

STD companies from near-certain oblivion, there was an outcry about the philistinism which was sure to follow. For years afterwards, old-time Sunbeam and Talbot followers insisted that 'their' marques had been ruined: the fact was that they could never have survived without a takeover, and that just happened to be by Rootes.

As my American friend and long-time collaborator Richard Langworth once most famously wrote in his earlier study of these cars:

> The Rootes family should not be looked upon as the villains our champagne-quaffing brethren who drive pre-war Talbots say they are: knaves who buried the grand marques of the golden past. The Rootes brothers simply did what was necessary, at a time of even greater economic perils than we English-speaking communities face today. They bought up defunct companies and put men back to work. And in time they began to produce some of the more interesting cars of the modern era.

SUNBEAM AND TALBOT – TWO NEW ROOTES-OWNED MARQUES

It is true that the Rootes Group had no intention of keeping old Sunbeam or Talbot models going for long once it had gained control. The market place, quite clearly, had already pronounced on that subject – Talbots might have been successful, but were expensive and sold slowly, while the public had virtually stopped buying Sunbeams.

Sunbeam of Wolverhampton had already slumped badly after their glorious 1920s period, and there was really nothing worth preserving. The only modern car in the range was the 1.6-litre four-cylinder Dawn (which had only just been introduced), the rest of the range being a close-knit group of modernized leftovers from the late 1920s.

Billy Rootes, the dynamo, the mainspring, the marketeer of the family (once he had gone Rootes drifted, rudderless, without a strategy or a new idea in sight) wanted Sunbeam and Talbot as prestige marques, but at the time even he didn't have a long-term strategy for their development. On the other hand, he did already control a prestigious coachbuilder in London – Thrupp & Maberly – so perhaps there was something to be gained by uniting names, operations and philosophies.

All that, of course, was more than twenty years before the Sunbeam Alpine was invented, and there were to be many changes of strategy connected with the Sunbeam name before it was properly – and separately – revived. In those two decades there were really several phases, only the last two of which made much commercial sense.

First of all, Rootes dabbled with reviving the marque by getting Talbot's design genius, Georges Roesch, to produce an eight-cylinder Sunbeam Thirty chassis, and hopefully to sell these cars with graceful Thrupp & Maberly bodies at high prices. Right away, therefore, it seemed as if Rootes was trying to bring Sunbeam, Talbot and Thrupp & Maberly together.

This failed miserably. The prototype Thirty was shown in 1936, but because Roesch had been obliged to use an existing Humber chassis, transmission and back axle, only lightly modified, and with its crude 'Evenkeel' independent front suspension still in place, it did not handle well, and did not behave at all like a thoroughbred. Only a handful of prototypes were built, and the project was abandoned in 1937 after Billy Rootes himself suffered a

Sunbeam – a famous motoring name

The Rootes Group did not buy the Sunbeam marque until 1935, by which time it had been building cars for more than thirty years.

The very first Sunbeam, of 1887, was a pedal cycle, made in Wolverhampton. From there it was a natural progression for Sunbeam to start making cars (from 1899), after which Sunbeam became an important car maker, which included settling the design of the 12/16 for mass military use in the First World War.

A merger with two French car-makers, Talbot and Darracq, meant the formation of the STD combine in 1920, though Sunbeam always carried on making its own cars in Wolverhampton, including a much respected twin ohc 3-litre model. But STD was incompetently managed, allowing technical chief Louis Coatalen to raise a large loan to finance Grand Prix racing activities, which effectively sowed the seed of financial disaster ten years before it came.

When that loan fell due for repayment in 1934, the money was not there. Rootes, along with Prudential Assurance, had already advanced further loans to STD to keep it afloat, and when that loan was defaulted, moved swiftly to make the combine bankrupt. A Receiver was appointed in the winter of 1934/1935, Talbot was annexed by Rootes in January 1935, and after a brisk fight with William Lyons's SS Cars concern, Sunbeam was also purchased in July 1935.

Thereafter, Rootes moved swiftly to close down the old Sunbeam concern, and to integrate the marque with Talbot of London, which had an altogether more illustrious reputation. Diehards, traditionalists and 'vintage' enthusiasts all hated Rootes for what was being done – though none of them were ready to admit that the only alternative seemed to be complete closure.

From 1938 Rootes therefore launched a new marque called Sunbeam-Talbot, cars which had special coachwork with a Talbot 'feel', but with chassis and all running gear based on those of current Hillmans and Humbers, and with assembly based at the Talbot factory in London.

After the Second World War, Sunbeam-Talbot assembly was moved to Coventry and sales expanded strongly, yet by the early 1950s these cars were being sold overseas as Sunbeams. At home the 'Sunbeam' name, on its own, was revived when the first Alpine of 1953 appeared, and the 'Talbot' half of the title duly disappeared at the end of 1954.

From 1955, and the launch of the Sunbeam Rapier, 'Sunbeam' once again became a fully fledged Rootes marque, its models always being the fastest and the most sporting of the complex model ranges built by the Group.

After the Alpine sports car was finally dropped in 1968, the Sunbeam marque carried on until 1976 when the latest corporate owner, Chrysler, killed it off. A year later, in 1977, 'Sunbeam' returned as a model name for Avenger-based hatchback models (including the Sunbeam-Lotus rally car), these cars finally being laid to rest in 1981.

chassis breakage when out on a test run; no hardware or physical evidence survived his wrath, for he demanded that the entire project be scrapped.

In the meantime, Rootes carried on building existing Talbots (which were being assembled at a factory in West Kensington), but ordered virtually no new components. This meant that as stocks ran down, the models' specifications were gradually degraded by the substitution of more Humber material, and in the end quite a number of Humber body pressings were also employed.

By mid-1937 the real Talbots had died away, the only remaining model being a 'Talbot 10', which used a small side-valve engine, and which was once succinctly described as a 'Hillman Minx in a party frock'. The Talbot factory at Barlby Road

Rootes rescued Sunbeam and Talbot in the 1930s, soon changing their characters and market aspirations. This was the Hillman Minx–based Talbot Ten of the late 1930s.

was beginning to look empty, and Rootes's investment was looking creaky, to say the least.

By this time, though, Billy Rootes had developed a better and very profitable new idea – better, that is, for his business and his shareholders, though not better according to the die-hards. In 1938 Rootes revealed the first of what would be a growing family of up-market sports saloons and convertibles which were dubbed Sunbeam-Talbots.

This was a classic Rootes example of corporate make-do-and-mend. The layout and design of the cars would be based on existing Rootes Hillman and Humber engineering, their bodies would, in the main, be supplied by a Rootes subsidiary called British & Light Steel Pressings of Acton, West London, while final assembly would be at the nearly empty Talbot factory at Barlby

Road, which was only three miles away.

SUNBEAM-TALBOT – A MARKETING SUCCESS

At this moment in its history, Rootes had established a very definite corporate character and 'image' for its cars. On the one hand, this meant that some people were happy to sneer at the engineering of its cars, but on the other almost everyone admired the way it set about its marketing programme.

In other words, technically Rootes cars had nothing to be proud of, yet the sales force and the dealer chain rarely seemed to have any problem in 'moving the metal'. At the end of the 1930s it didn't seem to matter that all the cars had side-valve engines (many other British cars were just the same), often dismal performance and unremarkable styling, for the prices were right, the dealer network was properly established, and the cars seemed to be very reliable.

The public might not have gone weak at the knees when it studied a new model from Rootes, but usually it thought it was getting value for money. Accordingly, when a couple of new side-valve-engined 'Sunbeam-Talbots' – one a Hillman Minx engined Ten, the other a six-cylinder Humber-engined 3-litre – appeared in 1938, the public took them at face value, and queued up to buy.

The fact that the smaller car was a much-modified Talbot Ten (which was,

itself, based on the mid-1930s Hillman Minx), while the larger car was a reworked 'Talbot 3-litre' (which was itself pure Humber apart from the stylish body) did not matter. As that much-missed historian Michael Sedgwick commented about the larger machine:

> The bodies were authentic Talbot, and in sports saloon guise the car looked the part but engine, gearbox, brakes, frame and wheels were equally authentic Humber...

A year later these original types were followed by additional Sunbeam-Talbots – 2-litre and 4-litre models (which were, respectively, based on the Sunbeam-Talbot

Rootes invented the Sunbeam-Talbot marque in 1938, soon offering four slightly different models behind the badge. This was the original Minx-derived Sunbeam-Talbot Ten.

Ten and the 3-litre, with different engines and longer wheelbases), which meant that Rootes had rather effortlessly invented a four-model range without spending a capital fortune. Rootes dealers beamed, while Rootes's accountants rubbed their hands.

Thus it was that the Rootes philosophy behind Sunbeam-Talbot – and, later, behind Sunbeam – was established. If Hillman was to be the mass-production badge, and Humber the solid, middle-class model, Sunbeam-Talbot was there to give Rootes the sporting image that it had so conspicuously lacked throughout the 1930s.

Commercially this was a successful venture. Before the production lines closed down at the end of 1939 (when the new marque had only been in existence for about fourteen months), no fewer than 5,402 of the Tens had been produced. No figures for the larger engined cars survive, but I will guess at about 500–1,000 cars.

As far as the diehards are concerned, this might have been automotive vandalism, but there is no doubt that it was a success. Faced with criticism, Rootes could always smile politely, then point to the fact that Barlby Road had never been busier, and that the new Sunbeam-Talbot badge was appearing at a faster rate on many more cars than either badge had ever adorned the earlier models.

THE 80 AND 90

Once the Second World War had been won, Rootes developed its three-marque family of cars – Hillman, Humber and Sunbeam-Talbot – even further. Although assembly at the Barlby Road factory was soon closed down, and all car assembly moved into the company's ex-aero-engine 'shadow' factory at Ryton-on-Dunsmore, just south-east of

Coventry, things carried on as before. To rationalize even further, Sunbeam-Talbot assembly was also concentrated on the vast (80-acre) Ryton-on-Dunsmore factory after May 1946.

Although Billy Rootes was still not ready to split 'Sunbeam' from 'Talbot', for his post-war models he actually allowed the specialization of Sunbeam-Talbot to go one stage further.

This time the new cars, when they appeared, would be allowed to have their own chassis, as well as special coachwork. While he was still determined to get the last ounce out of Rootes's investment in machine tools for building engines and transmissions in huge numbers, he even allowed his engineers to develop special engines for the Sunbeam-Talbots. This time, it seemed, he was ready to allow post-war Sunbeam-Talbots to look *and* feel different.

For the first three post-war years, Rootes decided to cut the complication of its pre-war range, and reintroduced the 1939/1940-type Ten and 2-litre models, both of which were based on the same chassis frame, though with different wheelbases.

As before the war, the four-door saloons wore all-steel body shells produced in the old-fashioned, cramped, British and Light Steel Pressings factory in Worple Way, Acton. Drop-head coupé shells, partly coachbuilt with wooden framing, were manufactured by Carbodies in Coventry, while the simpler but still coachbuilt tourers were produced by Whittingham & Mitchell in London SW6.

Then, in the summer of 1948, the new post-war cars, dubbed Sunbeam-Talbot 80 and Sunbeam-Talbot 90, were ready for sale. Once again these were an amalgam of old-style Rootes, rationalized engineering, specially developed engine modifications and special styling – and if you think I am labouring that point, consider the combination which eventually led to the design of the Sunbeam Alpine of 1959.

Then, as later, Sunbeam-Talbots looked smarter than any other Rootes car. Look back at Rootes's Earls Court Motor Show exhibits of 1948 and you would see old-style big Humbers (Super Snipes and Pullmans), square-rigged, Loewy-influenced new Hillman Minx and Humber Hawk saloons – and a pair of extremely sexy new Sunbeam-Talbots.

These cars, in fact, had been shaped by Ted White, who had started his working life as a body design engineer at BLSP.

He started working there well before the war [Roy Axe recalls] and was usually involved with a man called Ted Green. They had worked on the original Sunbeam-Talbot styles – in fact Ted Green dated right back to the Talbot Darracq days, and had joined Rootes as a consequence of the takeovers. Ted White had designed the original Sunbeam-Talbot Ten, and the 2-litre which evolved from it.

Ted, in fact, had not only styled but engineered the distinctive shape of the first Sunbeam-Talbot, which had no metal pillar between the rear passenger door and the rear quarter window, so the door glass closed on to the rear quarter glass. In side view it gave the Ten and 2-litre models a unique visual flavour.

After the war, the two Teds were then asked to do another Sunbeam-Talbot. Although American author, Richard Langworth, wrote in *Tiger, Alpine, Rapier* that the Raymond Loewy Studio was much involved in the shaping of Sunbeams and Sunbeam-Talbots, this was not evident in the 1948/1949 models.

Raymond Loewy was much involved with Rootes at that time [Roy Axe continues] and it has been written up in several places that Loewy was involved in the Sunbeam-Talbot 90. In actual fact he was not. It was always Ted Green's and Ted White's baby. In fact I'm told that the roof panel of that car – the Sunbeam-Talbot 90 – is actually the same pressing as that of the Sunbeam-Talbot Ten of 1938.

It was obviously an expensive press tool. Well, they kept that, and they built the lower part in the post-war fashion. Ted once told me that he was inspired very much by the shape of aircraft drop tanks [fuel tanks which could be jettisoned in mid-air] that had been used during the war, and that is where the front wing shape came from.

Thus it was that the post-war Sunbeam-Talbot evolved as a very different motor car from the other Rootes models on which it was based. The original 80s and 90s used a development of the existing 2-litre's chassis frame, which is to say that they were lumbered with old-fashioned beam axle front suspension, and a certain lack of torsional rigidity.

Mechanically they differed only in that the 80 used an ohv version of the existing side-valve Minx engine, whereas the 90 used a similarly modified version of the larger Humber Hawk engine. As you might expect, the saloon car shells came from British & Light Steel Pressings. BLSP also built the bare bones of the two-door convertible shells, which were then completed by Thrupp & Maberly in Cricklewood.

ENTER ALPINE, EXIT TALBOT

After two years the 90 was given an entirely new and special chassis frame, under a

By 1953 (this was the Earls Court Motor Show of that year), Sunbeam-Talbot was a completely integrated part of the Rootes Group – as was the Thrupp & Maberly coachbuilding concern. This stand shows a mix of big Humbers, Hillman Minx convertibles and Californian coupés, and a Sunbeam-Talbot 90 Mk IIA Convertible.

largely unchanged body style, this frame being a rigid new layout including coil spring independent front suspension. The original 80, on the other hand, had always been an under-powered failure, and was not continued.

Rallying experience, and success, then led to the 90 Mk II becoming the Mk IIA in 1952 but, more than that, it also led to the birth of the first-ever Rootes Sunbeam – the original Alpine two-seater. In name, but certainly not in technical pedigree, this was the true predecessor of all the later Sunbeam Alpines and Tigers which feature in this book.

Although this new car which, for clarity only, I will momentarily call a Sunbeam-Talbot Alpine, was aimed at the North American market, where Billy Rootes had great ambitions, its design was inspired directly by a British one-off – a rally car which had been built by the Rootes dealer from Bournemouth, George Hartwell.

As Lewis Garrad, later Number Two to his illustrious father Norman in the Rootes 'works' Competitions Department, once told me:

Hartwell was a very big man, over six foot three, strong, with tremendous courage and very little sympathy towards his cars. Actually he had very little sympathy towards anybody.

In 1952, he took a Sunbeam-Talbot 90 Convertible drophead and modified it by cutting the bodywork, creating a two-seater body. He also fitted two carburettors, and soon found out that with the extra torque, third gear would break like hell. George got very good at changing gearboxes.

After he built this car he brought it up to Coventry, and B. B. Winter [Rootes's technical chief] decided to build it. Here we had a really beautiful car. It was, I think, ahead of its time. To use it in rallying took a lot of work, but we got the basics right – the suspension, steering and gearbox – eventually.

The story of the Alpine's development, however, emphasizes the serious problems which Rootes had in developing a sports car, and a sporting image. Except for Norman Garrad, at the time virtually no one at Rootes had any experience of sports cars, or of sporting motoring; Garrad, of course, had been involved with the Talbot marque since the early 1930s. It was Garrad, I believe, who gave the car its name, for his 'works' 90 saloons had made quite a reputation for themselves on the French Alpine rally and Garrad was quite determined to use the new two-seaters on the same event in future!

Technically, the team, which was based at Humber Road, Coventry, didn't have a clue. Headed by Bernard ('B. B.') Winter, they only knew about mass production and executive cars – and pretty ordinary ones at that. Winter had been Rootes's engineering boss since the late 1930s (a period when talented young men like Alec Issigonis and Bill Heynes had rushed to get away from the stifling and mundane technical atmosphere at Rootes), and had never been an innovator. In fact he had started

his working life as a service engineer, then as a service manager, and did not even move into the Rootes Engineering department until 1935.

By the time the Alpine generation which concerns us came along, 'B. B.' was about to retire, which was probably just as well as his generation would surely have killed it off at birth. Remembered by old colleagues as a manager, rather than a designer, a faithful Rootes family acolyte rather than a forward-looking engineer, he was known to have little interest in fast cars which handled well or even looked good.

In addition, whatever his latter-day apologists might now suggest, Billy Rootes was a fully-paid up salesman, but a motoring philistine. He knew all about selling cars, had a great feel for the market place, particularly overseas, but knew nothing about sports cars or how they should be designed.

Predictably, therefore, the S-T Alpine's chassis was very much the same as that of the 90 saloons, and its final styling was influenced by several hands. The inspiration was certainly that of George Hartwell's 'special', Thrupp & Maberly (who produced the 90 Convertible, and would have to build Alpines) also had an input, and it was certainly scrutinized at the Loewy studio's headquarters in the USA.

In the end, the Rootes style, finalized by Thrupp & Maberly, was very close to that of the Hartwell prototype, and Billy Rootes was apparently delighted with it. To quote Roy Axe once again:

The Rootes family themselves were dominated by Billy Rootes. Without him, they were nothing. Everyone used to say, 'Billy's alright, but he's kept in his place by Sir Reginald, Sir Reginald is the key', but I didn't agree: Sir Reginald *wasn't* the man at all.

Billy was the marketeer, the dynamo. At the end of the war, when it was a case of 'Export or Die', especially to the USA, he really cottoned on to what was needed, better than any of his rivals in the motor industry, and he in fact pushed the sale of cars to the United States. He was acutely aware of the kind of car the United States customers liked and responded to.

Alpine Launched

And so it was that the two-seater Alpine first went on sale in 1953. Originally, in the spring of 1953, the Alpine was built purely for export to the United States, but from the autumn of that year, right-hand-drive cars for the UK and for some of the old 'Empire' territories, were also built.

Although it was really far too heavy to compete with smaller and more nimble cars such as the Austin-Healey 100 and the new Triumph TR2, the Alpine actually had a good, brief, though not sensational record in motorsport.

An early prototype achieved more than

Mike Hawthorn (famous racing driver) and Norman Garrad (in passenger seat) posing with the Alpine at the Earls Court Motor Show. Garrad always liked to persuade the rich and famous to align themselves with his cars.

The original Sunbeam Alpine of 1953 was a big two-seater tourer which was very closely based on Sunbeam-Talbot 90 / Sunbeam Mk III engineering. MWK 969 was a very early example used to set high-speed demonstration figures, both on the Jabbeke Road in Belgium, and here at Montlhéry banked circuit near Paris, where it covered 111.2 miles (177.9 km) in a non-stop hour's running. Leslie Johnson is at the wheel, Stirling Moss is leaning in to offer encouragement, and Competitions Manager Norman Garrad (in light suit) is close to the car's front corner.

Alpines of 1953 were effectively two-seater derivatives of the four-seater Sunbeam-Talbot 90 convertible. One result was that there was a long, but shallow, boot compartment.

120mph (193km/h)on the Jabbeke high-speed road in Belgium, repeating that trick at the French Montlhéry banked race track, while teams of rally cars were then used on the French Alpine rally, successfully enough for Stirling Moss to gain back-to-back unpenalized runs, and to win himself a coveted *Coupe d'Or* (Gold Cup) for three such drives in consecutive years.

Not only was the Alpine the first post-war Rootes car to carry the 'Sunbeam' badge, but it also inspired Rootes to drop the 'Talbot' half of the name from its 90 models. Before this time, in any case, Sunbeam-Talbots had been exported to some export territories with 'Sunbeam' badges, so rationalization was inevitable. Accordingly, from the end of 1954 the Sunbeam-Talbot marque was killed off, the Mk IIA became the Sunbeam Mk III, and a new tradition had been established.

Yet these were not the mass-market Sunbeams which Rootes needed to expand their glamorous export markets. They were too heavy, too specialized, and too expensive for that. Less than 28,000 90-based saloons, convertibles and Alpines were produced in nine years – an average of only around 3,000 cars a year.

By the mid-1950s, however, Billy Rootes had already moved to change all that. A new breed of car called the Sunbeam Rapier had arrived – and a different generation of Alpine was on the way. The original Alpine had been an 80bhp car weighing 2,900lb (1,300kg), which struggled to reach 90mph (145km/h): the next Alpine would be just as powerful, would be 750lb (340kg) lighter, and would always be able to approach 100mph (160km/h).

It was an exciting prospect.

2 Shaping the Alpine

In my opinion, previous studies of the Alpine have not started early enough. All of them have started with Ken Howes, with fins, and with the development of the shape, but that was months – years, perhaps – after the *idea* of a new Rootes sports car began to grow.

The fact is that the Alpine, as a project, took years to evolve, and was first considered in 1955, at about the time when the first of the 'Audax' family of cars (Minx/ Rapier/ Husky/ Gazelle) was being introduced.

Even in today's product-planning obsessed motor industry, a new breed of car (not merely a new version of the old) begins to take shape long before the stylists get their brief. It begins to evolve even before the planners start to lay down their ground rules - usually in the mind of one man.

In this case, it all started with Sir William Rootes, his pride and his restlessness. Irritated because the original Sunbeam (-Talbot) Alpine had been a commercial failure, and jealous of the headlines being garnered all round the world by Austin-Healey, MG and Triumph (particularly Triumph, I understand, for they were Rootes's largest competitor in Coventry at the time), he began to plot a rival.

RIVALS – AND RESPONSES

The development of British sports cars mushroomed in the 1950s. Our motor industry had got back on to its feet after the war, there was a seemingly endless demand for cars overseas, and in particular there seemed to be great opportunities in the bright and optimistic North American market.

MG and Jaguar were first to tap that rich vein of sales, but both Healey (soon to be Austin-Healey) and Triumph rapidly followed suit. By the end of 1955 the Austin-Healey 100/4, the Triumph TR3 and the MG MGA were making all the running.

Yet Rootes was lagging behind. The 'Talbot' Alpine had been ready before the Austin-Healey or the Triumph, but had been a commercial failure. The dynamic Sir William Rootes himself, his company's own best salesman, could not settle for the fact that the early-1950s Alpine had been too old-fashioned, too heavy and too expensive.

Worse, it had been developed by a team who really knew nothing about sports cars. Not even the learners at Triumph (who joined the sports car élite, from a standing start, in 1953) ever inflicted a 2,900lb (1,300kg) car with a sloppy steering-column gearchange on the public. Rootes, in other words, did not understand the sports car market in the early 1950s.

The problem was with the people rather than the facilities. Technical chief Bernard Winter knew all about Minxes and Super Snipes, and stylist Ted White was relying heavily on the advice he got from the Loewy Studio. Even Norman Garrad, whose rally team was successful (but not *that* successful in terms of major victories), was already middle-aged and was a traditionalist rather

Alpine – four different generations

Pay attention please! It's important to realise that there were four different generations of Alpine, and that the cars described in detail in this book were the second-generation models:

1953 – 1955: The Alpine roadster was an open two-seater version of the Sunbeam-Talbot 90 saloon/drophead coupé types, had a 2.3-litre four-cylinder engine and a steering-column gearchange.

1959 – 1968: These are the Alpines covered in this book.

1969 – 1976: The third generation Alpine was a de-tuned version of the Rapier/H120 fastback coupé model of the day, that car in turn being based on the Hillman Hunter saloon. Much less powerful and slower than the sports cars of the 1960s, it was a 90mph (144km/h) four-seater two-door car which left no trace of any character on motoring history.

1975 – 1985: Originally badged as a Chrysler Alpine, then from mid-1979 as a Talbot Alpine, this was a front-wheel-drive Anglo-French hatchback design, using a variation on the Simca 1100's transverse engine/gearbox layout in a new and rather larger shell. Alpines were assembled in Coventry from 1976.

It was badged as a Simca in France and some other countries. From 1982 - 1984, there was also a conventional four-door notchback style known as a Solara. To add marketing insult to injury, for the last two years there were special edition 'Minx' and 'Rapier' types.

than an innovator. From top to bottom, in what was a large Group, there was really no flair, and few young men were promoted far unless their family name was Rootes.

Sir William, at least, seems to have understood this. Roy Axe sums up well :

> Billy always seemed to know what he was doing. He was no fool, especially in business terms, and had always had that distinctive 'something'. Billy's ideas were usually good. He was often in the States, and he saw the reception given to the Corvette and the new Thunderbird. The feeling started to build up [and no doubt John Panks, a director of Rootes Motors Inc. in the USA, had an input] that a sports car was needed.

New Building Blocks

The car we now know as the Alpine, however, was merely one of a whole series of new cars which evolved from the same 'Audax' family, of which a new-generation Hillman Minx was much the most important member.

The first post-war Minx had been launched in 1948, using side-valve engines and transmission components which had all been designed way back in the 1930s. The first moves to replace this generation of cars were made in the early 1950s, and it was typical of Sir William Rootes's vision that he (and his brother, Sir Reginald) approved a truly colossal investment for the future.

The whole programme revolved around a new monocoque body/chassis unit (the four-door saloon was to be tooled and manufactured by Pressed Steel at Cowley), which had a 96in (2,440mm) wheelbase. There would be an all-new small ohv engine (the first totally fresh engine to be

Rootes's American ambitions

After World War Two, Britain was an exhausted country – physically, emotionally and financially. To keep paying for the war effort, the government had been forced to borrow billions of US dollars, and in the coming years would be obliged to pay them all back.

The British government therefore made sure that industry adopted an 'exports first, home market last' policy, and the British motor industry concentrated on selling cars to the USA.

This, together with a burgeoning styling link with the Loewy Studio, which helped to add some transatlantic touches to Rootes cars, meant that Sir William Rootes longed to expand his Group's North American sales.

But it wasn't easy. Early post-war Hillmans and Humbers were neither smart enough, nor fast enough, to attract much American interest. Like other British tycoons, too, Sir William was jealous of the success of MG and Jaguar sports cars in North America, and tried to fight back.

With that in mind, the original Sunbeam Alpine was launched in 1953, a two-seater which was closely based on the chassis and body style of the Sunbeam-Talbot 90 convertible type. All original production was reserved for the North American market, and it was so obviously aimed at that continent that it had a steering column gearchange, bench-type seats and whitewall tyres.

The 2.3-litre Alpine looked good, but struggled to get on terms with British rivals like the 2-litre Triumph TR2, and the 2.7-litre Austin-Healey 100, both of which were faster and a lot cheaper. Alpines of this type were only built for two years – 1953 to 1955 – and about 3,000 such cars were produced.

Sir William's ambitions, therefore, were frustrated, especially as the Rapier (which had the sort of style and colour/trim combinations which ought to have appealed to the Americans) was not a Transatlantic success either.

This, therefore, is where the idea of building a new type of Alpine was born. To beat the other British sports cars, Rootes would have to produce a smart two-seater in the same size, price and performance bracket.

designed at Rootes since the 1930s), with transmissions and a new coil spring front suspension to suit.

But that was not all. Rootes also planned five-door estate car and two-door convertible derivatives of the Minx, two-door coupé and convertible versions of a more-powerful machine to be badged as a Sunbeam Rapier, while there would also be a short-wheelbase (86in (2,185mm) – 10 inches (254mm) shorter than the Minx/Rapier types) three-door estate car called a Hillman Husky.

By any standards this was a massive programme and was going to take years to implement. Rootes had to accept a phased series of launches, which was going to take two or three years to complete. At that stage, in the early 1950s, I should emphasise that Singer had not even entered the reckoning, and that there were no firm plans to produce a sports car either.

The ohv engine, a 43bhp/1,390cc unit, was revealed at the end of 1954, just in time to be used in the last versions of the existing Minx models. The very first of the new-generation cars – actually it was the Rapier coupé – was launched in October 1955, and the most important derivative of all, the Hillman Minx saloons and convertible, appeared in May 1956.

By that time Rootes had taken over Singer (which was in any case about to collapse financially) and a Singer Gazelle derivative had been added to the master plan, which would appear later in 1956. The last of all the originally-planned machines, the short-wheelbase Husky

Minx, Rapier and Husky – a new mid-1950s generation

After the post-war Hillman Minx was launched in 1948, Rootes gave it a very profitable seven year run. Then, in the early 1950s, a strategy was laid for the next decade or so. First of all, it was time to design a new engine for the Rootes medium sized cars, and next there would be a new generation Minx.

For the mid-1950s, though, Sir William Rootes was more ambitious than ever before. Instead of asking his designers merely to create a new Hillman Minx, he also wanted them to make provision for a short-wheelbase Husky, an up-market Sunbeam (to be called Rapier), and a two-seater sports car (the Alpine).

Unexpectedly, too, there was more. Even before the new generation Minx was revealed, Rootes had also rescued Singer from bankruptcy, which allowed a Singer-engined version of the new car – the Gazelle – also to join the new family.

All cars used the same basic coil spring/wishbone front suspension, the same worm-and-nut steering and the same live axle/leaf spring rear suspension, but although the basic unit-construction platform was the same for all models, there were many important detail differences. To allow for all this complication, the following basic 'building blocks' were laid down:

Wheelbase 96 inches:

> Four-door saloon (Hillman Minx, Singer Gazelle)
> Five-door estate (Hillman Minx, Singer Gazelle)
> Two-door coupe (Sunbeam Rapier)
> Two-door convertible (Hillman Minx, Singer Gazelle, Sunbeam Rapier)

Wheelbase 86 inches:

> Two-door estate car (Hillman Husky)
> Two-door sports car (Sunbeam Alpine)

Engines used for original models were:

> Rootes 1,390cc/40bhp (Hillman Husky)
> Rootes 1,390cc/47.5bhp (Hillman Minx)
> Rootes 1,390cc/62.5bhp (Sunbeam Rapier)
> Rootes 1,494cc/56bhp (Singer Gazelle - 1958)
> Rootes 1,494cc/78bhp (Sunbeam Alpine - 1959)
> Singer 1,497cc/49bhp (Singer Gazelle)

– by any standards, this was a massive new project, and financially the most ambitious Rootes had ever tackled.

estate car, was finally introduced in January 1958.

Inventing the New-Generation Alpine

All the historical evidence points to the *idea* of a new Alpine taking shape in 1955, with the packaging and styling car taking place more than a year later.

Sir William Rootes and his advisers were determined to make up for the commercial failure of the first Alpines by producing a new generation. However, whereas all the

Alpine engine – a major Rootes 'building block'

When the Rootes Group took shape at the beginning of the 1930s, three all-new engines were designed. The smallest of these, intended for use in the original Minx, was a simple, rugged, side-valve four-cylinder unit of 1,185cc/30bhp, with bore and stroke of 63mm × 95mm.

This engine was so rugged, so reliable, so cheap to build, and so successful, that it stayed in production for 26 years, until 1957. By that time the capacity had grown to 1,265cc, and an ohv version had been developed for use in the Sunbeam-Talbot 80 model, but it had reached the limit of its development.

Early in the 1950s, therefore, Rootes began the design of a new generation of small/medium four-cylinder engines, to take over from the ancient side-valve unit. Apart from the early engines all using cast iron cylinder blocks and heads, the two designs were totally different, as this comparison shows:

Detail	1930s Minx engine	1950s Rootes engine
Year introduced	1931	1954
Cylinder head	Side valve	Overhead valve
Swept volumes	1,185 (1931)	1,390cc (Original)
(cc)	1,265 (from 1949)	
Bore and stroke	63 × 95mm	76.2 × 76.2mm
(mm)	65 × 95mm	

Not only this, but the new engine was always intended to have a long and extremely varied life. Still in use until the 1980s, it would eventually grow to 1,725cc, would be produced with cast iron and aluminium cylinder heads, with a whole variety of carburation, and eventually with a five-bearing crankshaft.

Compared with the old engine, the new unit was a much more stocky unit with a shallower block, rather longer than before, for it had a much larger bore and a shorter stroke, and there was space for a certain amount of 'stretch' in future years. The crankshaft was stiff and sturdy, with large main bearings, and there was a significant overlap between main and big-end bearings to add to the stiffness of the shaft.

Actuation of the overhead valves, by long pushrods and rockers, was strictly conventional, the valves being vertically placed in modified 'bath-tub' combustion chambers.

The original engine of 1954 had a cast iron cylinder head, though a totally different aluminium head would be developed later in the decade, initially for use in the Sunbeam Alpine, and its close technical relative, the Rapier saloon/convertible type.

British competition – the 100/4, the TR3 and the MGA – used unique chassis frames not shared with any other car in their groups, Rootes chose another method.

To save time (and money !), the approach already used by Alfa Romeo (with the Giulietta) and Fiat (the 1200 Cabriolet) was chosen. Instead of designing a new separate chassis, the new Alpine would have unit-construction based on the modi-fied pressed-steel platform of an existing family car.

But there was more. There never seems to have been any doubt in their minds that the new car had to be a lot lighter, smaller and faster than the original car, which meant that it had to be an evolution of the new 'Audax' range of cars.

As the world now knows, the Alpine then took shape around a much-modified version of the short-wheelbase Husky's floorpan, whose wheelbase was only 86in (2,185mm). Ideally, for packaging reasons, that wheelbase ought to have been a bit longer, but this would have meant carving up the Rapier/Minx underframe at great cost.

This is how the dimensions of the Alpine's major British competitors stacked up:

Model	Wheelbase (in)	Overall length (in)
Austin-Healey 100/4	90 (2,286mm)	151 (3,835mm)
MG MGA	94 (2,388mm)	156 (3,962mm)
Triumph TR3	88 (2,235mm)	151 (3,835mm)

Roy Axe, later to become Rootes's chief stylist and to go on to complete further distinguished assignments at Chrysler UK, Chrysler USA, Rover, and then to found his own design consultancy, has an important story to tell about the development of the Alpine's shape, but first confirms most peoples' thoughts about the wheelbase:

It was always developed on the Husky wheelbase and, yes, it was very short and rather cramped for us. There was a lot of emphasis on fins, because this was an era where Chrysler was doing a lot of fins in the USA, and Billy Rootes had certainly seen these at Motor Shows.

Would it have been easier to shape the car on a longer wheelbase?

It probably would, but I think it was always a good sports car in the Rootes image. It was always seen as a very ele-gant motor car. It was a well-proportioned car that stood the test of time, even to today, because it still looks really quite nice.

Accordingly, once it was agreed that the rather short Husky platform had to be used, the basic architecture of the new vehicle was soon settled. The Husky platform was already intended to accept the running gear of the new 'Audax' range, so it was very easy to specify the engine, the transmission and all the other running gear of the most powerful version – the Sunbeam Rapier.

Styling Personalities at Rootes – and the Loewy Connection

When the time came to start work on shaping the new sports car, Rootes found itself in a terrible dilemma. Should it try to do the job 'in house', or should it hand it over to its long-term styling consultants, the Raymond Loewy studio? Should it even try to have the car shaped by a completely different personality?

In those days, the mid-1950s, the Rootes styling studio was situated in the old Humber Road factory, and was placed above and beyond the main experimental workshops. I visited this department several times in later years, and although it had been smartened up a little by Chrysler (after they took a stake in Rootes), it was still small, cramped, and not at all conducive to the shaping of modern, elegant, new cars. The miracle is that in the years it operated, the department *did* manage to produce a series of practical, useful and commercially successful machines.

Apart from one department at Ryton which produced wooden models, all the styling – drawings, renderings and mock-up work – was concentrated at Humber

This was the Rootes Group's Humber Road complex in Stoke, Coventry – in fact a developed version of two originally independent businesses, Humber and Hillman. This shot is taken facing east, which means Coventry's city centre is behind the aeroplane taking the picture. The design, engineering and styling departments are in that long white-faced line of buildings on the extreme left of this shot. The 'works' competitions department buildings are on the right edge of the cricket ground, close to the chimney.

Road, a long way down a narrow driveway with experimental workshops and design drawing offices on one side, faced by production machine shops on the other side.

The main studio was upstairs, above an experimental workshop. There was an area where the stylist/designers worked, a separate office for the manager – Ted White – both alongside a showroom which included a turntable. In later years this was expanded by building out at roof level.

By modern standards – even the standard Rootes (later Chrysler UK) occupied at the Whitley facility – this was truly primitive, but it still felt glamorous enough of its day. Cars – prototypes, mock-ups, or plasticine/clay models – all had to be brought upstairs by lift, and for a prototype to be viewed outdoors it had to be taken downstairs, then trucked out on to the company's sports field. At the time, though, it was par for the course among British companies.

By the mid-1950s Ted White had been moved up to Coventry from British & Light Steel Pressings in London to be the department's manager, and to take over from Ted Wilks, the previous head.

Wilks had recently walked out on the Rootes family. This was not unusual, for Billy Rootes was never known to negotiate with anyone, preferring to lay down the law and expect immediate obedience. His public image, well-honed by his Public Relations people, was as the tireless, patriotic, all-knowing, world-conquering entrepreneur, but in private he could be rude, impossibly demanding, and dictatorial.

The entire Rootes family tended to treat non-family members like lesser beings, always addressing them by their surnames, treating quite senior managers as vassals, and generally letting everyone know what their place was. [As one long suffering Rootes man once told me: 'Which usually meant that we were in the wrong !'.

There is mystery about White's move, for Ted was more of an engineer than a stylist, and was never likely to mix well with the Rootes styling coterie, who tended to be of what I call the 'purple handkerchief, drainpipe trousers and suede shoes brigade'. These people tended to be mocked by the earthy, dirty-fingernail artisans they had to pass on their way down the drive every morning – then, as later, neither seemed to understand, or care about, the others' points of view.

'Mind you,' one old hand told me, ' the Raymond Loewy gang used to be even worse, because they would come visiting with lots of gold medallions, bangles – all that stuff !'

However, it is now known that Ted White had somehow 'blotted his copybook' down at British & Light Steel Pressings, but no one ever spelt out what this was, and the well-liked White took the secret with him to his grave. Many lesser men would have been dismissed on the spot, but because of the sterling work which White had done on the Sunbeam range he was moved up to Coventry.

Ted White took his BLSP associate Ted Green with him, though Green, who was always closely connected with Humber styling and body engineering, never became involved in the Alpine project. Remarkably, Ted White would survive his disgrace (whatever it was) for more than a decade, would eventually become Director of Styling, and would hand over to Roy Axe at the end of the 1960s when the Alpine and Tiger projects had been wound up.

So, by 1955/1956, the two Teds had arrived at Humber Road, to manage and control the Styling department, and at the same time to co-operate with the Loewy Studio, which had a long-term design/styling consultancy agreement with Rootes.

Raymond Loewy himself was an expatriate French designer long resident in North America who had set up an industrial design house which styled everything from Gestetner copying machines to electric shavers, buses to ocean liners – and cars – before the outbreak of the Second World War. [Incidentally, a previous author of a book on Alpines insists on calling this man 'Loewry'....]

By the late 1930s Loewy had done some much-acclaimed work for Hupmobile and Studebaker, then opened a London office, where the Rootes connection was founded in 1938, with Clare E. Hodgman as manager. As Hodgman later told my American colleague, Richard Langworth: 'This was the Rootes brothers' policy. They wanted an American influence in their cars, something that would be fresher than what they had in England at that time.'

Hodgman also insisted that Loewy's

influence on Rootes was never a 'deciding factor', and that his office always worked with and alongside, rather than against, Rootes's own stylists. Ted White was responsible to Bernard ('B. B.') Winter in Engineering, though approval of all new shapes had to come from the Rootes family, all of whom were convinced that they were great stylists, and all of whom insisted in making minor changes to prototypes before signing them off.

Although certainly not in the concept, there was much detail Loewy influence in the style of the earlier Sunbeam-Talbots - the 80, the 90, the Mk III and the Alpine. The new-generation Minx and Rapier styles, however, were predominantly Loewy influenced.

As Studebaker expert Langworth points out, the original Rapier of 1955 was very clearly related to the 1953 Studebaker, for there were many touches borrowed or clearly evolved from the Starliner hardtop. The Mk II Rapier, styled in 1955/1956 at about the time work on the new-generation Alpine was due to get under way, was even closer to the Studebaker shapes – Hawks, this time – for both had upright grilles, concave tail fins, upright tail-lamps and a rich and colourfully upholstered range of interiors.

Shaping the New Car – 1957

There was no doubt in Sir William Rootes's mind, as 1956 ended, that he knew that he had no one in his own styling studios who could match what was being done by MG, Triumph or Austin-Healey. With an eye to selling cars in North America, he decided that he needed someone with a bit more flair than the White/Green duo. The Raymond Loewy team had to be consulted.

At this point Ken Howes enters the story. Howes, who had spent several years with the Loewy team (see the panel on page 33) was currently with Ford in Detroit. When Sir William Rootes talked to Clare Hodgman about the work he wanted done, Howes's name was mentioned, and Rootes decided to interview him.

According to Howes, he was eventually approached via John Panks of Rootes Motors Inc. of New York, and Bob Bourke, Studebaker's chief designer, was also involved. He flew to London to be interviewed, in Devonshire House in London's Piccadilly, by the intimidating quartet of Sir William, Sir Reginald and Geoffrey Rootes, plus B. B. Winter.

Hired just as soon as he could get his release from Ford USA, Howes arrived at Coventry with the title of Assistant Chief Appearance Designer, but with rather a

Bernard ('B. B.') Winter was Rootes's technical director from the 1930s until the 1960s. In general, he did not have sporting inclinations, but it was his team which laid out the Minx / Gazelle / Rapier / Husky family from which the Alpine of 1959 was evolved.

Kenneth Howes

As far as the world of motor car styling is concerned, Ken Howes was a one-car phenomenon. Although other members of the team, notably Geoff Crompton and the young Roy Axe, also had much to contribute, Howes is usually credited with the style of the Sunbeam Alpine of 1959.

Ken Howes originally trained as an engineer with the Great Western Railway in his native Swindon, worked for a time in that company's design offices, before joining the London office of the Raymond Loewy studios in 1948. By this time, of course, Loewy was already a consultant to Rootes on car styling matters.

In four years based in London, he not only worked on many industrial (i.e. non-automotive) projects, but was involved in Loewy work for the Austin company, including preliminary proposals for what became the Austin A30. As Howes later admitted, from 1948 to 1952 he worked on styles for soap, perfume packaging, clocks and cookers!

Then, in 1952, he moved to Loewy's New York office, then to South Bend, Indiana, where he worked on Studebaker styles and interiors. In 1955, though, he moved to head up a design group at Ford of Detroit, before being head-hunted by the Rootes Group to generate the Alpine style, where his official title was Assistant Chief Appearance Designer.

His work at Rootes, which began in early 1957, is detailed more broadly in the main text, but his stay in Coventry was short-lived. Following what appears to have been a major row with the Rootes Family (all of us who have experience of the Rootes Group in this period know that this was not difficult!) who were reluctant to give him personal credit for the car, he left to set up his own design consultancy.

Thereafter he worked on industrial designs – as he once said, he always thought it important to strive for eye-appeal or: '...a beauty of form and colour that created in the consumer the desire to possess.'

In spite of the grace of his Alpine, he never again seems to have accepted commissions for other automotive work, and by the end of the 1960s had virtually dropped out of the motoring scene.

For more than forty years Rootes's London HQ was in Devonshire House, in Piccadilly, opposite the Ritz Hotel. The executive offices were upstairs, for there was an extensive, and glossy, showroom on the ground floor.

Sports cars – the marketplace in 1957

When the Sunbeam Alpine was conceived in 1957, mainly with an eye to sales in the USA, three British sports cars were already well established in that market.

These were :

The Austin-Healey 100-Six, a 2.6-litre/6-cylinder engined development of the original Austin-Healey 100, which had first gone on sale in 1953. It had detachable sidescreens and four-wheel drum brakes. A higher powered version was imminent. The top speed of the existing car was around 103mph (165km/h), and the British retail price was then £1,144.

The MG MGA, a 1.5-litre/4-cylinder engined car, which had been introduced as recently as 1955. It was still at the beginning of a long development life, was fitted with detachable sidescreens, and four-wheel drum brakes. The MGA's top speed was around 98mph (157km/h), and the British retail price was £996.

The Triumph TR3, a 2.0-litre/4-cylinder engined car, which had been developed from the original TR2 of 1953. It had detachable sidescreens, but front-wheel disc brakes had recently been standardized. A facelifted car (the TR3A) was imminent. The TR3's top speed was about 102mph (163km/h), and the British retail price was £1,021.

Accordingly, Rootes (who were obliged to use a 1.5-litre Minx/Rapier type of engine) projected a new car with a top speed of as close to 100mph (160km/h) as possible, but to be better-equipped, more modern-looking, and to have wind-up windows.

and in 1959

By the time the Alpine was put on sale, all Rootes's rivals had upgraded their products, so this was the situation in the important USA market at the beginning of the 1960 Model Year:

Austin-Healey 3000	$3,051
MG MGA 1600	$2,444
Sunbeam Alpine	$2,595
Triumph TR3A	$2,675

– clearly the Alpine was carefully priced, to fall between the MGA and TR3A levels. Rootes had high hopes for it.

nebulous position. Roy Axe, then a junior member of the design staff at Humber Road, recalls that:

He was not a Rootes employee, but a consultant, and in the initial stages he was still part of the Loewy organisation. Ken was brought in, in a very peculiar reporting position. I don't think many of us really knew who he reported to – except direct to Billy Rootes.

This made the organization of the styling department even more difficult than usual to understand. Howes, it seems, bypassed Ted White in most of his dealings with The Family. White, for his part, reported to George Payne, who was chief body engineer, while Payne in his turn reported to B. B. Winter, who then reported to the Rootes family. It is easy to see why the arrival of Howes made several other people feel uneasy.

Howes was hired for only one purpose, to shape a new sports car which became the Alpine. His assistants on the project were

Geoff Crompton (not Jeff Crompton, as identified elsewhere, neither was Geoff his boss), an ex-art school graduate who already had a great deal of styling experience, and a young Roy Axe:

> That was the entire team at first, though Ron Wisdom later joined the team to work on detail. Geoff's wife, Pauline, was also working in the department at the time, on paint and trim aspects.

If this seems to be an absurdly limited team for what was a major project, let me outline the way that Rootes cars took shape in the 1950s – the way that I personally saw in many styling departments in the 1950s and 1960s. There were probably no more than six designers on the staff at the time, who would start every project by producing sketches.

Once a basic theme had been agreed, that would then have to be worked up into a scale drawing, with major sections shown, before a scale model was produced. Usually this would be a quarter scale, or perhaps a one third scale, in the form of a wooden buck, into/onto which plasticine (later a special modelling clay) was moulded.

At that point the model would be viewed in the studio by the Rootes family, who would often check dimensions and curves by referring to the scale drawing. Once that was approved, full-scale drawings would be prepared, with many more cross-section and long-section lines developed, before these were sent downstairs for the woodworkers to make a full-size car in wood.

To ensure that cars like the late-1950s Minx convertible were rigid enough, they had a much reinforced floorpan, and this knowledge and technology helped enormously when the time came to develop the Sunbeam Alpine of 1959. This range of Minx models shared the same basic front and rear suspensions, plus running gear, as the Rapiers and other models in the 'Audax' family.

Until the Alpine was developed, the Sunbeam Rapier was the fastest and most sporting car in the entire Rootes range. This particular car is a Rapier III of 1959, which shared the vast majority of its chassis and mechanical components with the new Alpine.

In the 1950s, the first Rootes prototype bodies were always erected in the department underneath the Styling studio in Humber Road. This, in fact, was a late 1940s Hillman Minx, but the general layout of what was a cramped department did not change for many years!

This wooden mock-up would be amazingly functional, for the doors would open and close, and there would be correctly shaped cabins and engine bays – the advantage of wood, in sections, being that changes could be made easily, and quickly.

That car would then be painted [Axe details] and placed on the turntable in the studio, where The Family would look at it. They would then insist on making changes – Billy in particular – they would say take a quarter of an inch off here, change that radius there. One of the woodworkers would then appear with his spokeshave and plane, and alter the profile, usually in their full view.

The car would then be repainted, reviewed, and possibly altered again. This process went on for a long time, and it was not until the Rootes family was satisfied that the very first metal car was made.

Development of the new Alpine shape went on for much of 1957, with both Howes and Crompton working away at it. There is still healthy disagreement as to who did most of the work – certainly it was not all to the credit of Howes, nor did Crompton do as little as some people suggest. Roy Axe, at least, agrees that he was little involved in the concept, but looked, learned, helped, and absorbed every detail of what was proving to be a fascinating project.

A quarter-scale style had already been produced (it was Crompton's work) but not liked, so Howes started again from scratch. Apart from the Husky wheelbase and platform being of fixed dimensions, there were no restrictions:

No pictures of Alpine clay models seem to have survived, but this mid-1960s shot of the Rootes Styling studio at Humber Road shows the cramped conditions in which staff had to work. Those are early studies of the Avenger model. Security, as you can see, consisted of a high wall between the factory and a terrace of houses in suburban Coventry!

Same cramped studio, same impossibly cramped conditions – and this is a 'see-through' mock-up of the Sunbeam Rapier which would be announced in 1967, just before the Alpine was finally killed off. Would you like to be confused? There would also be an Alpine version of this fastback four-seater.

Very different looking machine, but a blood brother of the Alpine, this was the Commer Cob, a light commercial derivative of the Hillman Husky estate car. Both cars shared the same short-wheelbase platform and general chassis layout on which the Alpine would be based.

It was looked on as a completely new car that would be a break with the past [Howes later said] It was basically an intuitive design. I wanted a sports car that would be ahead of the competition – projected slightly into the future. I wanted it to look fast, to have a clean, sculptured form, without ornamentation, and to have a good aerodynamic shape.

Happily, Rootes planners had already decided that the new Alpine should have features that its rivals lacked, notably a bowed windscreen, wind-up windows and (hidden away) front-wheel disc brakes, so Howes's vision of a 'slightly into the future' style would be upheld.

Having seen the way that other cars have suffered from the 'too many cooks' syndrome, I can see how relieved Howes, Crompton and Axe must have been to develop their own ideas without interference. The design certainly came together relatively quickly, for even the original models looked much as the final style would.

From the very beginning this was a car whose theme included a relatively low front end, with headlamps in the corners, and with a waist line which rose relentlessly towards the rear where it ended with a pair of fins. On the very first car there were different styles on each side (this was, and is, quite usual), with a deep scallop on the flank on one side, but a plain wing shape on the other.

The point of the scallop started just behind the door shut-face, widened as it progressed rearwards, and surrounded the extremities of a proposed tail lamp/indicator cluster on the tail.

Fins like this, which were still not yet at the absurd heights which would follow, had first evolved at Chrysler, under Virgil Exner's influence, and one only had to look at cars like the 1957 Chrysler Windsor (which came complete with a massive scallop in the flank, widening towards the tail-lamps) to see where that Alpine feature came from.

Roy Axe remembers that this feature stayed in the original Alpine style throughout 1957, but that in the end the Rootes family decided that it preferred a plain flank instead. It was definitely significant that this was the same year in which the highly-decorated Vauxhall Victor had been introduced to a torrent of abuse from motoring writers and arbiters of style – Sir William Rootes always had extremely sensitive antennae, and this was one influence which persuaded him to retreat from such flamboyance.

Well before the end of 1957 the finalised Howes/Crompton style was ready for approval. Scale models had been tested in the MIRA wind tunnel with gratifying results. Rootes never had such a feature – indeed it only ever expressed a passing interest in drag coefficients, certainly when the author was in the Coventry area at this time.

The final viewing took place in the styling studio in Humber Road, where the mock-up, which had been painted Carnival Red and given as much brightwork as possible to make it look as lifelike as a non-runner could be, was placed on the turntable. Having fussed over it, criticised it, and altered it several times in recent months, the main phalanx of The Family were finally ready to approve it.

As ever, on these occasions, Sir William Rootes was always ready to take the credit for the work himself, which must have been infuriating for the designers who had spent so much time satisfying his every whim. This time, however, there was not only approval, but the comment that Howes had done a good job.

The first Kenneth Howes Alpine shapes featured deep scallops along the flanks, behind the doors, but were otherwise remarkably similar to the finalized designs.

This is a very early Alpine prototype, probably pictured in 1958/1959. Note the strange hardtop style, which was not adopted for production, the extra driving lamps (useful for when this car had to be driven hard and fast, overnight, to build up mileage way from prying eyes), and a scoop in the bonnet.

Well posed, and giving a different view on things, this shows that there was a great deal of space behind the seats in the new Alpine, even if it would be wrong to call it a '2+2'.

To be strictly accurate, it was only at this stage that the Alpine got its name, for Howes had originally wanted to call it a Sunbeam Sabre, and for quite some time it had merely been known by the few who were privy to the secrets as 'the new sports car'.

Design – Who, Why and Where?

In the meantime, the design and evolution of the new car's running gear had been forging ahead at Humber Road. Basically, this was done by surveying all the engine, transmission and chassis work which had already been completed, or proposed, for the still-new Sunbeam Rapier coupé, and improving on that.

B. B. Winter's family-car-orientated team of engineers, who were thoroughly familiar with the step-by-step improvements for which Rootes was famous, take all the credit for what was achieved at that stage.

Although two other talented engineers (Peter Ware and Peter Wilson) later had a great deal of influence on the Alpine, and its development, the Tiger, neither had yet

RAS 436 was a fictitious registration number on this prototype, but at least it signals the link between Rootes and Armstrong-Siddeley which were so strong at this time. This is a running prototype, in 1959, still with what appears to be mock-up tail-lamps and – naturally – no badges.

41

come on to the scene, so could take no credit for the original layout.

The Rapier, of course, had been the first of the wide-reaching 'Audax' Rootesmobiles to appear, yet it was really no more than an offshoot of the latest Minx/Gazelle/Husky range, and certainly did not have a separate pedigree. However, even in the early stages, the 1,390cc-engined Rapier had more power than any other version of these cars, and after only one season that engine was boosted still more, from 62.5bhp to 67bhp (gross). For this car, too, Laycock overdrive was standard, though the suspension was still floppy, and a steering-column gearchange was still fitted.

By the end of 1957, when the Alpine style was settled, the already-revised Rapier Series II was ready for launch, with a 68bhp (net)/1,494cc engine, recirculating instead of worm-and-nut steering, a stiffened-up front suspension and (Praise be!) a floor gear change instead of 'four-on-the-tree' like the original car.

The Series II Rapier, on which original Alpine mechanical studies had been based, went on sale in February 1958 but by this time Rootes, being Rootes, was already planning for a Series III derivative, which was to be introduced in the autumn of 1959.

For the SIII there was to be a whole raft of promising technical developments, which would change the Rapier from a 'nearly car' to something more formidable and worthy of the 'sports saloon' description.

For the engineers who were beginning to work on the Alpine, it was all rather encouraging. Not only would there be yet

WDU 427 was a mid-1959 Coventry registration plate, and this was an early example of the finalized Alpine, which we later came to know as the Alpine I.

another increase in power – from 68bhp to 73bhp – but this was to be achieved with a brand new aluminium cylinder head having more logical and efficient porting.

There would be closer-ratio gears, and all this extra performance (the SIII Rapier could reach 92mph) was to be kept in check with Lockheed front-wheel disc brakes. Not only that, but a new hypoid-bevel rear axle design was also on the way.

Once Sir William Rootes had approved the new Alpine project, naturally he was in a tearing hurry to see it come to the market place. Ideally he would have liked to see the car break into the North American market early in 1959, but there simply wasn't time to get the design frozen, the testing complete and, most critically, the body press tooling made ready in time for that.

Not that Sir William always let practicalities get in his way. Roy Axe and his associate Rex Fleming have both told me that they dreaded Sir William's visits to London Motor Shows because :

He would come back full of enthusiasm for something he had seen on a rival's car, and want something like that included in our cars before the next Show! If that meant making changes to a body pressing, that left only, say, eleven months between the "Good Idea" and making the first production cars.

Pressed Steel would usually say it could not be done in the time but Billy, being Billy, usually got his way in the end.

The 'eleven month rule', though, could not possibly be met, with an all-new body style, so Sir William realised that with a style settled in December 1957, he could not expect to see production cars being built before the middle of 1959. Even so, every month lost to his rivals irritated him

beyond measure, and the engineers were constantly being urged to get the job done early.

Long-serving Rootes (via Singer) man Johnny Johnson, and later Alec Caine (ex-Fedden), became Project Engineers on the Alpine project, which meant that they headed up the development team and were the conduit of all information, problems, and news between the designers and the cars themselves, the actual team of development engineers and drivers including characters like Don Tarbun and Bernard Unett (Unett, of course, would eventually become better known as a racing driver, both of Sunbeam Tigers, Hillman Imps and 1970s Chryslers).

In the meantime B. B. Winter approached his retirement date, and within months two tall, lean, laconic, and very different types of engineer – Peter Ware and Peter Wilson – arrived to freshen up the team. The scene was now set for Rootes to accomplish a definite, if gradual, change to its image: not only was the Alpine being developed, but to follow it there would be a new range of rear-engined saloon cars (the Imps) and, after that – who knew?

Where to Make the Cars ?

Well before the style was settled, the manufacturing problems had been tackled. The previous-generation Alpine, based closely on the Sunbeam-Talbot 90 layout, had been made at Ryton, in and among the Sunbeam saloons and convertibles, from bodies finished off by Thrupp & Maberly, but for the new-generation car this was not feasible.

For the new-type Alpine, not only did somewhere have to be found to manufacture the unique two-seater body shells, but space – a lot of space – also had to be found to paint and trim them, then turn them into complete motor cars. Because Rootes's only

Armstrong-Siddeley – the Coventry connection

Although the Rootes–Armstrong-Siddeley tie-up over the manufacture of Sunbeam Alpines is well-known, the first business links were made some years before this contra-deal was signed.

Armstrong-Siddeley of Coventry came into existence in 1919, when two other organisations, Armstrong-Whitworth and Siddeley Deasy, merged. Throughout its life, this marque of car was really a sideline for a company which made most of its money by building aeroplane engines. The cars were always built in a rambling factory complex at Parkside, to the south of Coventry's centre.

After the Second World War, Armstrong-Siddeley was was one of the first to introduce new models, by building a series of six-cylinder cars, the 16hp and 18hp types, known as Hurricanes, Lancasters, Typhoons and Whitleys. All these cars used developed versions of the 1930s Armstrong-Siddeley engines, with the usual choice of pre-selector gearbox or synchromesh transmission.

These cars gave way to a new and larger car called a Sapphire, which had an advanced 3.4-litre six-cylinder engine featuring part-spherical combustions and a cross-pushrod valve gear layout. Once again, this car was offered with pre-selector transmission, or with a four-speed manual gearbox.

This time, however, there was a difference. The post-war 16hp/18hp types had used Armstrong-Siddeley made manual gearboxes, but in this case the manual transmission was supplied direct from Rootes in Coventry. This was a four-speed all-synchromesh type, operated by a steering-column gearchange, and was normally used in the Humber Super Snipe of the period.

This was the first actual business connection between Armstrong-Siddeley and Rootes, though the two companies would become much closer in future years.

Later in the 1950s, as described more fully in the text, Rootes and Armstrong-Siddeley got together in an ingenious 'contra' deal, with Armstrong-Siddeley developing and manufacturing Sunbeam Alpines, and Rootes redesigning and redeveloping the Sapphire-type six-cylinder engine for use in its own new-generation Hillman Super Snipe.

assembly plant, at Ryton-on-Dunsmore, was not equipped to make body shells – it was only able to make complete cars from complete shells – there was no place for the Alpine.

In any case, by 1957 the Ryton plant was already bursting at the seams, making more than two thousand Hillmans, Singers and Humber family cars every week, and even if the body shells could have been sourced elsewhere, to insert a more limited number of sports cars into what was essentially a family-car plant would have been an irritant.

For the very first time, therefore, Rootes decided to farm out Alpine assembly to another plant, to an outside contractor. Thoughts of building the cars at Thrupp & Maberly in North London had already been

suppressed, as was the idea of using the old-fashioned Singer premises in Birmingham (which Rootes was planning to clear, and convert into a parts warehouse). The solution was found much closer to home – at the Armstrong-Siddeley company in Coventry.

As detailed in the panel above, Rootes already had strong links with Armstrong-Siddeley, which operated from a large if rambling factory complex at Parkside, close to the city centre and only about four miles from Ryton-on-Dunsmore. Although this company was heavily – and profitably – involved in making gas turbine (jet and turbo-prop) and rocket engines for military aircraft, by 1957 sales of Armstrong-Siddeley cars were falling away rapidly.

Because Rootes was also looking around

Almost there, and almost ready for introduction – this was WDU 427, a finalized Sunbeam Alpine I.

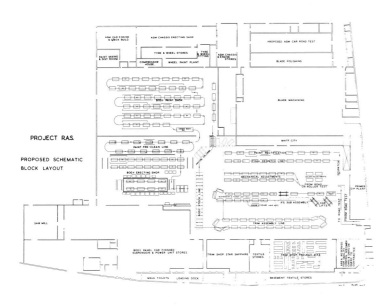

PROJECT R.A.S.

PROPOSED SCHEMATIC
BLOCK LAYOUT

This rarely-seen planner's drawing of a factory floor shows the way that a large section of the Armstrong-Siddeley factory in Coventry was rejigged to manufacture the new Sunbeam Alpine in 1959. Body shells were welded together at centre left, painted at top left, then trolleyed through to the main assembly, inspection and checking lines at centre right. Armstrong-Siddeley car assembly was squeezed into tiny spaces, mostly at the top left corner of this plant. The 'Blade machining' and 'Blade polishing' references were to Armstrong-Siddeley departments which were devoted to making Sapphire jet engines for military aircraft like the Hawker Hunter.

This picture shows
that Rootes and
Armstrong-Siddeley
invested heavily to
produce jigs and
welding fixtures
which would manu-
facture Alpine body
shells. Front end sub-
assemblies are
stacked in the left
foreground, rear sub-
assemblies on their
tail fins to the right
of the welding fix-
ture, with underbody
platforms on the edge
of the shot, extreme
left. The main assem-
bly lines are in the
distance, under the
'No Smoking' sign.

This rather confused picture shows the Alpine final assembly area at the Armstrong-Siddeley factory in Coventry, where the cars were all assembled between 1959 and early 1962. More significant is the view, in the foreground, of the underside of the Alpine's body shell, which is temporarily fixed to a pole on a rotating 'spit'. It demonstrates the ruggedness of the cruciform brace, and also shows the deep box which housed the battery, which lived under the padded platform behind the right front seat.

for ways to enhance its Humber ranges – and thought Armstrong-Siddeley could help – it therefore struck an enterprising co-operative deal with the Coventry concern. On the one hand Armstrong-Siddeley would help develop a new Rootes six-cylinder engine for use in the next Super Snipe – an engine which just happened to be a close copy of the Armstrong-Siddeley Sapphire design (if you don't believe me, look at cross-section and other drawings for proof !) – while in return Rootes would hand over much of the development, and all the initial manufacturing, work on the new Sunbeam Alpine.

At a very early stage, therefore, the Alpine took on a new so-called secret code, the RAS sports car – Rootes Armstrong Siddeley. Although the car's design was completed at Humber Road, much of the prototype testing was based on the Armstrong-Siddeley experimental department at Parkside.

Then, as later, though, Coventry was not a city which could hold secrets for long. As a young man, working in the city (at Jaguar) at the time, I soon learned that something out of the ordinary was brewing at Parkside. The sports cars seen flitting in and out of the works were certainly not Armstrong-Siddeley models, and once a few familiar Rootes faces had been seen with them, or driving them, the cover was blown.

Armstrong-Siddeley then redeveloped much of the Burlington Works section of Parkside (the name related to the Burlington-branded car body shells which had been made there between the wars) so that the Alpine could take precedence over its fast-dying 'own-brand' models. A factory floor plan scheme, which is on page 45, shows that the vast majority of floor space was allocated to the Alpine, with remnants of Armstrong Siddeley Star Sapphire tucked in to any corner which was still available.

This major programme occupied most of 1958, and the first half of 1959, while development and testing of the new sports car was completed. By mid-summer of 1959, therefore, the Alpine was ready to meet its public.

Peter Ware

After joining Rootes in 1958, then becoming Director and Chief Engineer of Rootes from 1959 to 1966, Peter Ware was intimately connected with the birth, production and development of the Alpine and Tiger models. Along with his friend and associate, Peter Wilson, he had much to do with lightening up the previously dour Rootes technical team.

Peter was born into an engineering family in 1918, for his father had been Chief Engineer of Straker-Squire in Bristol before joining Vickers in Sheffield, which was Peter's birthplace.

After joining the Navy through Dartmouth Royal Naval College, he served in the Navy before joining Roy Fedden at Bristol Aeroplane Co. Ltd. After working on the Fedden car project, then at Dowty, and finally at CAV (Electrical), he was head-hunted by Rootes (Roy Fedden recommended him), taking over from B. B. Winter when that long-serving Rootes personality retired.

Although he always admitted to being far too busy to enjoy driving the many prototypes which his team developed in his eight years at Rootes (Peter Wilson, no mean driver, did most of that for him) he was a hands-on engineer with very high standards. In many ways he dragged the team away from its former rather stodgy attitudes, to taking up a more forward-thinking approach – just right for a company which was getting more and more into sporting cars.

Like other top men at Rootes, the arrival of Chrysler in the mid-1960s was unsettling, so when a lucrative offer came from Dunlop, to manage the new engineering division, he took it. He finally retired from the motor industry in 1977.

Peter Wilson

Like his mentor, Peter Ware, Peter Wilson joined the Navy at eighteen (in 1937), working his way up from Dartmouth, where he met Peter Ware for the first time. Later he became a Fleet Air Arm pilot after the war, and eventually became a part-time racing driver, eventually becoming a 'works' driver for Bristol (in the 450s in various events including Le Mans) and BMC (in an MGA in the Tourist Trophy).

Having left the Navy in 1957, ranked as a Commander, he worked for Aeroparts in Hereford for a time (a few years earlier, they had made body shells for the Healey Westland sports car), before getting the call from Peter Ware to join him at Rootes.

Within 12 months he had taken over the running of the experimental departments, a position which he held down, with various titles, for the next two decades. More than any senior manager on the site (Mike Parkes, being a relatively junior employee, doesn't count !) he was a driver of considerable ability, fast and very safe, and with the sort of competition record behind him that brooked no argument when he commented about a new car's roadholding or balance.

Aloof and offhand with those he thought didn't understand the subject, but kindly and encouraging to those (the author included) he seemed to like, Peter Wilson was popular with his peers, yet misunderstood by many who knew him little.

He retired from Chrysler (which had absorbed Rootes at the end of the 1960s) at the very end of the 1970s, just after helping to force the new Sunbeam-Lotus project through the system. It was once said that only he and Des O'Dell (who inspired its birth) truly understood the car, and that few other Chrysler engineers would go near it!

3 Alpine I and II – Fashionable with Fins

Getting the new Alpine from the drawing board to the production line wasn't as easy as it looked. It wasn't just a case of gutting a Rapier III, stuffing everything into a new body shell, then pressing the button. Especially for a motor industry engineer, life is never as simple as that.

Keith Duckworth of Cosworth once famously remarked that: 'Development is only necessary to rectify the ignorance of designers' – a sweeping statement which can only be justified by a genius like Keith if he controls every aspect of a programme. In 1958 and 1959, when the Alpine programme was coming together, problems appeared where none had been expected.

The first was that the design of the shell had to be settled, and all the pressings for making it in quantity had to be commissioned. Shells for the prototypes - eleven of them - were made with the help of Abbey Panels of Coventry (the same resourceful 'metal bashers' who did so much for Jaguar, particularly in producing bodywork for the D-Types and – soon – for the E-Types).

However, once testing had begun, it was clear that the open-top shells were simply not stiff enough. Shorn of its metal roof and the stubby all-metal cage around the cabin, the Husky-based platform and inner panels could not cope. The only solution, much resisted by the planners because it added complication to the design *and* put up the cost, was to weld an X-brace cruciform member under the platform, making sure that there was a big hole in the centre of the 'X' to allow the propeller shaft to be threaded through it.

Even then, that was not the end of the problem. Prototypes still suffered from body vibrations, which might have been acceptable to engineers used only to running rugged, hairy-chested, wind-in-the-hair sports cars – but not to Rootes engineers whose standards were higher.

Technical director-elect Peter Ware was alerted to the crisis, took out B. B. Winter for a drive, after which the two agreed that further stiffening of the engine bay was going to be needed. Changes to the inner wing/wheelarch panels could not be entertained (for these were standard Hillman Husky/Hillman Minx items), and tooling for the new bulkhead/firewall was also well-advanced.

The only answer – later described to me by Peter Wilson as 'a blacksmith job' – was to fit a pair of diagonal strengthening stays between the arches and the bulkhead itself. Latter-day rally engineers would recognise the location as that of the front-strut braces of a modern roll cage, though in this case the struts were bolted, rather than welded, at each end. This was done so that the struts could be removed prior to removing the engine upwards through the body shell.

Peter Ware, such a civilized man who

hated being the bearer of bad tidings, later said of B. B. Winter that: 'He was such a charming man that I hated upsetting him, but I just could not allow the car to go into production like that.'

BUILDING THE SHELLS – A THREE-DIMENSION JIGSAW

Although the Alpine's structure took shape around the Husky's pressed-steel 86in (2,185mm). wheelbase platform/underbody, a car which had gone on sale in January 1958, it was nevertheless a complex shell to assemble, because several contractors provided different sub-sections.

After a great deal of deliberation, Rootes planners arranged for shell assembly to take place at the Armstrong-Siddeley factory in Coventry, which meant that the Burlington Plant therefore came close to being a complete manufacturing unit, as opposed to merely an assembly plant.

As every Alpine owner and enthusiast knows, the basis of the Alpine's monocoque was the underside of the Husky, complete with its inner wheelarches and some other structural fittings. This section was pressed and welded together at Cowley, near Oxford, by the Pressed Steel Co. Ltd, who also added the unique cross-bracing

For the first three years of its career, the Alpine had assembly facilities all to itself, at Armstrong-Siddeley. This was the final inspection line for completed cars – the bright strip lights were needed to reflect any imperfections on the body panels.

cruciform sections which rough road testing had shown to be essential.

Several other major sub-assemblies were then provided to be welded to that underbody, one being a combined bulkhead and bonnet sides, another embracing the front wings, front section and scuttle panel which dropped over the first item, and a third then being the rear end pressings, rear wings and closing panels. The final major items, of course, were the doors themselves.

Because Rootes had no spare pressings capability of its own (BLSP and Thrupp & Maberly were fully committed at this time), these sub-assembly jobs were mainly contracted out to Joseph Sankey of Wellington, in Shropshire.

Looking back, to commit Alpine body assembly to Armstrong-Siddeley of Coventry was a very brave move, for that concern had never before tackled anything like it. Building bespoke body shells for Armstrong-Siddeley cars was one thing, but these had all used separate box-section chassis frames. Rootes, however, had invested heavily in welding and jigging facilities, as archive pictures shown in this book confirm.

Geoffrey Rootes, the first Lord Rootes's eldest son, ran the Group's manufacturing operations for many years, before succeeding to the family title when his illustrious father died in 1964.

The original production car of 1959 in all its glory, complete with badging and optional white-wall tyres. On the first cars there was only a short support at the front edge of the wind-up door glass, and the petrol filler cap was a plain, round, creation...

The factory layout at Parkside shows that shell assembly took up considerably less space than that of the paint shop and that, naturally enough, final assembly took up most space of all. When the Alpine shells had been welded together, protected against corrosion, and painted, they then began a tortuous journey down assembly lines, first being trimmed, then having all their running gear added, and finally going down lines which looked after adjustments, paint rectification and any other work needed before they were driven out of the building and on to transporters.

Alpine I running gear

The first Alpine production cars (which we can now call Alpine I) were built in June/July 1959, about three months before the original Rapier III models were produced at Ryton. Most of the innovations already planned for the Rapier in 1957/1958, therefore, were seen first in the Alpine, which made many people think that the Alpine had inspired the Rapier III, rather than the other way round.

In fact there were many detail differences between Sunbeam Alpine I and Sunbeam Rapier III running gear. Both cars shared the latest version of the 1,494cc four-cylinder engine, for which a new aluminium cylinder head had been prepared: both had a 9.2:1 compression ratio, and shared the same camshaft.

However, whereas the Rapier used a simple cast iron exhaust manifold, and a full oil bath air-cleaner to the twin downdraught Solex carburettors, the Alpine used a more efficient tubular exhaust manifold, and because of bonnet clearance restrictions, only used flame trap covers over the carbs. The differences were small, but significant:

...whereas the Alpine II, which appeared in the autumn of 1960, had a full-length window-glass support, and a three-eared filler cap, but no other changes.

Alpine I (1959 – 1960)

Numbers Built :
11,904

Layout
Unit-construction body/chassis structure, with steel panels. Two-door, front engine/rear drive, sold as two-seater open sports car, with optional steel hardtop.

Engine

Type	Rootes
Block material	Cast iron
Head material	Cast aluminium
Cylinders	4 in-line
Cooling	Water
Bore and stroke	79 × 76.2mm
Capacity	1,494cc
Main bearings	3
Valves	2 per cylinder, operated by in-line overhead valves, pushrods and rockers, with camshaft mounted in block, driven by chain from crankshaft.
Compression ratio	9.2:1
Carburettors	2 Zenith 36 WIP2.
Max. power	78bhp (net) @ 5,300rpm
Max. torque	89.5lb/ft @ 3,400rpm

Transmission

Four-speed manual gearbox, with synchromesh on top, third and second gears. Optional Laycock overdrive on top and third gears.

Clutch	Single dry plate; hydraulically operated

Overall gearbox ratios

Top	3.89
3rd	5.41
2nd	8.32
1st	13.01
Reverse	16.48
Final drive	3.89:1

Overdrive (Laycock) was optional, on top and third gears, when the final drive ratio became 4.22:1. Overall transmission ratios were:

Top (O/D)	3.39
Top (direct)	4.22
3rd (O/D)	4.72
3rd (direct)	5.88
2nd	9.04
1st	14.13
Reverse	17.90
Final drive	4.22:1

Suspension and steering

Front	Independent, coil springs, wishbones, anti -roll bar, telescopic dampers
Rear	Live (beam) axle, by half-elliptic leaf springs, hydraulic lever-arm dampers
Steering	Recirculating ball
Tyres	5.60-13in cross-ply
Wheels	Steel disc, bolt-on, or optional centre-lock wire spoke
Rim width	4.0in

Brakes

Type	Disc brakes at front, drums at rear, hydraulically operated
Size	9.5in. diameter front discs, 9 × 1.75in rear drums

Dimensions (in/mm)

Track	
Front	51/1295
Rear	48.5/1232
Wheelbase	86/2184
Overall length	155.25/3943
Overall width	60.5/1537
Overall height	51.5/1308
Unladen weight	2,136lb/968kg

Car	Peak power (bhp @ rpm)	Peak torque (lb/ft @ rpm)
Alpine I	78 @ 5300	89 @ 3400
Rapier III	73 @ 5400	83 @ 3500

The low profile of the bonnet pressing also meant changes to the cooling system, with the Alpine being treated to a cross-flow radiator and having a separate (cast) header tank sitting atop the thermostat water outlet to the cylinder head.

The latest close-ratio version of the four-speed gearbox was specified on both cars (these ratios would not be shared by other Audax-generation cars for some time yet), and on the Alpine an electrically-operated Laycock overdrive which worked on third and top gears was optional, as it was on the Rapier.

The major difference was at the rear of the car, where the Alpine was the first to use a newly-developed hypoid bevel back axle. Within a year or so this would be adopted on all other cars in the 'Audax' family, but for moment it was unique to the Alpine. The final drive ratio was 4.22:1 if overdrive was fitted, or 3.90:1 if it was not.

Apart from special spring and damper settings for this, the lightest car in the 'Audax' family, the front and rear suspension layouts were the same as those used on family cars in the range. The massive pressed steel front-suspension crossmember was the same, as was the layout and geometry of the front anti-roll bar (whose arms were fixed to the forward arm of the front wishbones), and the steering gear, where the recirculating ball steering box was fixed to the bulkhead.

As on the Husky, but *not* as on the current Rapier/Minx/Gazelle types, there were lever-arm dampers at the rear. Telescopic dampers, no doubt, would have been a desirable fitting, but there was a certain lack of space to fit them, and in any case it was desirable to retain the standard Husky pressings and fittings at this point.

By being announced ahead of the Rapier III, the Alpine I also became the first such Rootes car to be fitted with front-wheel disc brakes, and even here there were differences from Alpine to Rapier. Problems, heartache, testing and detail investigation had led to Rootes choosing a Girling installation for the Alpine. Strangely enough (though I am certain that company politics, and long-term commercial dealings, were involved) the Rapier III got Lockheed brakes instead. As usual on all these cars, the handbrake lever was mounted on the floor pan, close to the outside edge of the driver's seat.

The Alpine was the first car in this family to use 13in diameter pressed-steel road wheels (those on Rapiers, Minxes and Gazelles were still 15in diameter), and there was an option of centre-lock Dunlop wire-spokes. In both cases, 5.60-13in cross-ply tyres were standard.

It was typical of this period in Rootes's history that a lot of thought had gone into equipping and kitting out the interior. The fold-back soft-top was much more civilized, and easy to furl and unfurl, than most of the rival models. Amazingly, though, instead of merely covering the folded-back soft-top with a plastic or leather bag, Rootes chose to provide three fold-down steel flaps. Not only were these heavy, fiddly, but expensive to tool, and once the familiar Rootes up-dating processes began they would not survive.

A steel bolt-down hardtop was optional, though few of these seem to have been ordered on the initial batch of cars.

In spite of the fact of the ultra-short wheelbase, a notional two-plus-two interior was provided, though the separate front seats were in stark contrast to the lightly upholstered shelf behind them. The 'plus

Right from the start, Alpines were available in open roadster (in the background), or hardtop (foreground) forms. The use of headlamp hoods was always a controversial feature, but Lord Rootes was convinced they were needed for the USA market.

No challenge here for restorers! These were the plain, but functional, door trim details on the orginal cars. Note the very limited support for the window glass, which would be changed in the autumn of 1960.

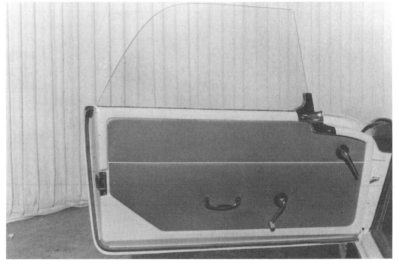

two' area, in any case, was useless for carrying people, for there was only 3.5in behind the front seats when they were pushed all the way back, which meant nowhere to put feet: the cushion was only lightly padded, the backrest being vertical and unpadded!

The nicely-equipped facia/instrument panel made up for this. There was a full range of Rapier-style instruments, with the speedometer and rev-counter sitting ahead of the line of the two-spoke steering wheel. As you might expect in a Rootes car (though not in some other sports cars), not only was the heater standard, but it actually worked quite well.

Although there was much Rapier under the skin, there was a totally different driving position, with a near vertical steering wheel (which would have encouraged a

The Alpine always looked best from a low aspect. This Series I car, pictured in 1995, has the optional 13in wire-spoke wheels which were so popular.

Like the Sunbeam Rapier of the day, the Alpine originally had a twin-carburettor engine, but because of the very low bonnet line there was room only for very simple flame-trap covers over the carburettor venturis. Note the simple but effective stiffening tubes connecting the inner front wheelarches to the scuttle/bulkhead panel.

straight-out leg position if had not been mounted so low), and good protection from the wind by a full-size screen and wind-up windows.

Even today, nearly forty years after the event, I can clearly recall driving an Alpine for the very first time, and being rather startled. At that time, not only was I used to the Sunbeam Rapier (as a rally car), but had often sampled both the MGA and the TR3A. The Alpine felt somehow more solid than other sports cars (the monocoque construction helped), with a softer and more 'touring' type of ride than any of them.

Considering the speed at which it had evolved, and the fact that this was the first real Rootes sports car, the Alpine was an appealing prospect. The Alpine, at least,

A 1959 Rootes publicity shot shows the so-called 'occasional' rear seat of the Alpine though, in truth, this was really no more than a padded shelf, as leg-room was virtually non-existent.

Until 1963 and the arrival of the Alpine III, there was an insultingly small amount of luggage accommodation in the boot of the Alpine, for the spare wheel, and the shelf covering it, took up most of the space. The towing hook on this car is an extra.

was not merely a 'me-too' concept, for it had features yet to be developed by its opposition and certainly it was a remarkably refined machine. So what would the public think?

Meeting the Press – and the Public

Although Rootes had decided to launch the Alpine on 2 July (an event preceded by glamorous functions at Cannes, in the South of France), PR supremo John Bullock's plan to achieve blanket coverage received a knock only a few days before that date. Due to a strike in the printing industry, both of Britain's 'establishment' magazines – *The Autocar* and *The Motor* – were forced off the bookstalls, and would not return until mid-August.

Not that Rootes needed to make any excuses, for the Alpine was keenly priced. Cheaper than any of its obvious rivals – at £971.55 the Alpine undercut the MG MGA by £25, and the TR3A by a useful £49 – it was also better-equipped in many ways. Incidentally, if you think £49 is not much, I remind you that the optional overdrive was

priced at £60.20, and very popular it was, too. BMC did not even offer an overdrive on the MGA – then, as later, no-one could understand why.

It was interesting to see that, when the Rapier was up-dated to Series III specification in September, the non-overdrive variety was priced at £986, just £14 more than the Alpine. So – was it worth paying £14 more, for two seats more, and a definite loss of performance? Rootes liked to set that sort of conundrum at all levels of its range.

A dozen pre-production cars – XVC 1 to XVC 12 – were earmarked for the launch, and the world's press gave the new arrival a very friendly reception. Armstrong-Siddeley had been recruiting assembly workers for some time, but soon found that it had to add a night shift at Parkside: this was even though deliveries to the USA did not start until the autumn of the year, by which time the 'selling season' was almost over.

The Autocar was the first to publish a full test with performance figures, writing about XVC 7 in September. This car, in overdrive form, recorded a mean top speed

The 'Alpine' script did not figure at the front of the new car, which was dominated by reference to the marque – and the Group which owned everything!

The Alpine's air intake looks smooth and efficient, doesn't it? It was only later, when Le Mans race cars were being prepared, that the engineers realised that most of the engine bay's cooling air had to find its way in from the underside of the car.

of 98.4mph (157.4km/h) but only 91mph (146km/h) in direct top) and, more importantly, overall fuel consumption of 25.5mpg (11.1l/100km).

The testers, who had made obfuscation and double-speak almost an art form at this time, clearly decided that there was too much 'touring' and not enough 'sports car' in the Alpine's character, commenting that:

> The standard of ride and control are such that the performance may be used to the full – and a spirited performance it proves to be...The ride is splendidly matched to the car's character...There is some roll on

corners taken really quickly, but it is firmly limited... Cornering fast is fun, for there are no tricks waiting to catch the unwary, and no appreciable tyre squeal... [However] Considerable practice and dexterity were needed to stow the hood in less than three minutes: the more important task of getting the hood up quickly was easier.

The summary confirmed earlier impressions : 'It is attractive, stable, safe, and unquestionably fast in spite of the emphasis placed on long-distance comfort. The world's markets are overdue for such a car.'

The Motor took XVC 9 through five

European countries before publishing its test in November, though I believe the driving was completed at least two months before publication. Then, as later, *The Motor* liked to keep well away from The Autocar....

Boasting that they had completed 2,000 (3,200km) miles during the test, the writers clearly managed to loosen up the engine a little, for this was slightly faster than *The Autocar*'s example – a one mph higher top speed, and 2.8 seconds quicker to 80mph (128km/h). Infuriatingly for Rootes publicists, however, *The Motor* recorded a top speed of 99.5mph (159.2km/h) – near, but not quite near enough, to the magic 100mph top speed which the factory wanted so much to advertise.

Once again the 'touring' aspects were emphasised for this was thought to be a car which: '...offers two people greater comfort than they would enjoy in many quite expensive touring cars... Some buyers might actually prefer rather firmer damping of the springs', and there was more faint praise of this type in the summary.

Autosport decided to hold back publishing its thoughts on XVC 7 (the same car which *The Autocar* had already used) until 23 October, its special 'Motor Show' number. John Bolster's opening remark set the tone of the whole test:

'Just once in a while, a car is produced that is better than it has any right to be ! Such is the Sunbeam Alpine.'

There was more of the same – much more – the highlighting of the maximum speed of 102.29mph (163.66km/h), unreserved praise for the roadholding and :

'The Sunbeam Alpine is a very attractive car, both in appearance and performance. It is as smooth and quiet as a typical medium-sized saloon, but there the resemblance ends. Though it rides well, it handles like a real sports car....'

For Rootes, though, whose ambitions in North America were naked and aggressive, it was much more important to get a favourable response 'over there'. *Road & Track* finally published its thoughts in May 1960 – getting on for a year after the car had first been shown to the European press.

Jumping to the last sentence, Lord Rootes must have been relieved to read that:

'The Sunbeam Alpine is a happy compromise for the buyers who want the sports car feel and a few creature comforts too (for two). In a country [USA] such as this, already pre-conditioned to the "personal car", it should find many a happy home.'

Road & Track had tested not one, but two different cars, one of them a hard-top model, but: 'The quality level of panel fit and finish varied considerably between the two.' It was significant that the best car came from Rootes's West Coast press office, the other being a private car which had not been specially prepared.

Another paragraph proved just how easy it was to rack up the price of a car in the USA for:

The basic price of the car, as quoted in the data panel at $2,645, obviously doesn't include the overdrive, which retails at $160. Our test car was equipped with white sidewall tyres (Dunlop Gold Seal) at $35, fresh air heater at $60, wire wheels at $105, tonneau cover at $39 and the hard-top at $260. Rootes Motors Inc. makes no charge for inland freight, if any, and this is paid for by the selling dealer. The car as tested, then, will go "out of the door" for $3,144, plus tax and licence in the Los Angeles area.

[Using an existing parity of $2.80 to the pound, this equates to £1,123 – cheaper than the equivalent car in the UK, but then there was no purchase tax to be paid in the USA.]

BUILDING A REPUTATION – WHAT TO DO NEXT?

Those were the days when I was working in Coventry, and when it was very easy for young enthusiasts like myself to get together with engineers from other firms. Motor clubs like the Coventry & Warwickshire MC and the Godiva CC were thriving, engineers like Lewis Garrad of Rootes often dropped in for a noggin or two, while team drivers such as Peter Harper sometimes turned up too. Mike Adlington, who not only worked on Alpine development and testing, was also a keen young racer – so we all learned a lot, but said very little !

In 1959 and 1960, therefore, it was easy to get the consensus of opinion about the new Alpine – and there were few disagreements. Almost everyone thought it was a smart car – sexy, even – but that it wasn't really fast enough. The fact that it was made by Armstrong-Siddeley, whose management wouldn't have recognised a sporting image if it had tripped them up in the corridor, didn't help, but there was this overall aura around the car of being good, but not yet quite good enough.

Perhaps we were all expecting too much. As a co-driver, I was used to turning up on rallies to see the first twenty numbers occupied by TR3As, and wondered why there were no Alpines. I saw my friends swanning around in MGAs, but not in Alpines. On the other hand, I started to see Alpines where sports cars had previously been absent – at the local golf clubs, and in the car parks of exclusive Midlands hotels. What was going on?

Rootes's marketing people, for sure, knew exactly what was going on. As expected, they knew they would have to do more to build up the Alpine's sports car reputation. Somehow, without spending a fortune (which wasn't available, in any case), they had to emphasize the Alpine's performance without losing any of its original qualities.

One way – the obvious way – was to get Alpines involved in motorsport. The other was merely to follow the path at which Rootes was already expert – to work away at all the details, and make a good car better. The first 'works' Alpines started racing in 1961, with quite remarkable results, but before then the basic design had already moved on. Only fifteen months after it had been launched, the original type gave way to the Alpine II.

Alpine II – a Makeover

By the end of the 1950s Lord Rootes had encouraged his staff to get involved in a process which still made their rivals feel nervous. Rather like the American companies, every year Lord Rootes wanted to have something new to boast about: he wanted his sales force to be able to boast about a new engine, a new style, or just a new package of features.

Once launched, the Alpine, just like the Sunbeam Rapier, the Singer Gazelle or the Hillman Minx, came in for that treatment. It makes life interesting for the historian, but must have been extremely wearing for the engineers and production staff who had to cope with it.

By the end of 1959 Alpines were flowing out of Parkside in ever-increasing numbers, but back at Humber Road the engineers were finalizing a completely new medium-size car range (the Hillman Super Minx/Singer Vogue family), along with a further-enlarged engine to suit.

From the start-up of Alpine II production there was a full-depth window glass support at the front end of the doors.

When the soft top on an Alpine was folded back, there were three hinged panels to move temporarily forward so that it could be stowed out of sight.

Alpine II (1960 – 1963)

Numbers Built :
According to Chassis Numbers, 19,956, though about 2,000 numbers seem to have been missed out during the move from Armstrong-Siddeley assembly to Ryton-on-Dunsmore assembly.

Layout
Unit-construction body/chassis structure, with steel panels. Two-door, front engine/rear drive, sold as two-seater open sports car, with optional steel hardtop.

Engine

Type	Rootes
Block material	Cast iron
Head material	Cast aluminium
Cylinders	4 in-line
Cooling	Water
Bore and stroke	81.5 × 76.2mm
Capacity	1,592cc
Main bearings	3
Valves	2 per cylinder, operated by in-line overhead valves, pushrods and rockers, with camshaft mounted in block, driven by chain from crankshaft.
Compression ratio	9.1:1
Carburettors	2 Zenith 36 WIP2 (later 36 WIP 3).
Max. power	80bhp (net) @ 5,000rpm
Max. torque	94 lb/ft @ 3,800rpm

Transmission
Four-speed manual gearbox, with synchromesh on top, third and second gears. Optional Laycock overdrive on top and third gears.

Clutch	Single dry plate; hydraulically operated

Overall gearbox ratios

Top	3.89
3rd	5.41
2nd	8.32
1st	13.01
Reverse	16.48
Final drive	3.89:1

Overdrive (Laycock) was optional, on top and third gears, when the final drive ratio became 4.22:1. Overall transmission ratios were :

Top (O/D)	3.39
Top (direct)	4.22
3rd (O/D)	4.72
3rd (direct)	5.88
2nd	9.04
1st	14.13
Reverse	17.90
Final drive	4.22:1

Suspension and steering

Front	Independent, coil springs, wishbones, anti -roll bar, telescopic dampers
Rear	Live (beam) axle, by half-elliptic leaf springs, hydraulic lever-arm dampers.
Steering	Recirculating ball
Tyres	5.90-13in cross-ply
Wheels	Steel disc, bolt-on, or optional centre-lock wire spoke
Rim width	4.0in

Brakes

Type	Disc brakes at front, drums at rear, hydraulically operated
Size	9.5in diameter front discs, 9 × 1.75in rear drums

Dimensions (in/mm)

Track	
Front	51/1295
Rear	48.5/1232
Wheelbase	86/2184
Overall length	155.25/3943
Overall width	60.5/1537
Overall height	51.5/1308
Unladen weight	2,219lb/1,006kg

Even with the ever-restless Lord Rootes demanding annual changes, it took time to convert a good idea into reality. Because changes to a car's shape meant costly and lengthy modifications to press tools this was never tackled lightly, and few other mechanical changes could be made at less than six to nine months' notice.

The package of changes which eventually appeared in the Alpine II of October 1960 were therefore 'signed off' by the early spring, which meant that they had been done when the original car had only been on sale for a few months.

The major change was to the engine, which was enlarged from 1,494cc to 1,592cc. Although the Alpine was the very first Rootes car to inherit this larger engine, it was already destined for use in other Rootes cars – for the Rapier SIIIA in April 1961, for the new Singer Vogue in July 1961, then with other Hillmans and Singers following later in the year.

To gain the extra capacity, the cylinder bore was enlarged from 79.0mm to 81.5mm, but the 76.2mm stroke was not changed. As expected, this made little difference to peak figures :

Car	Peak power (bhp @ rpm)	Peak torque (lb/ft @ rpm)
Alpine I	78 @ 5300	89 @ 3400
Alpine II	80 @ 5000	94 @ 3800

Although larger-choke Zenith carburettors were fitted (30mm instead of 28mm), because there had been absolutely no change to the aluminium cylinder head, the valves, porting or the camshaft timing, in some ways this was 'Much ado about nothing'. For a 6.5 per cent capacity increase had led to a mere 2.5 per cent improvement in peak power, and only 5.6 per cent more torque.

Power and torque curves issued at the time of launch (but beware – like every one else, Rootes issued idealised, rather than actual shapes at this time) showed that there was more torque throughout the range, particularly at lower engine speeds.

Rootes, however, went out of their way to emphasize that the 1.6-litre package also included a stiffened crankshaft, larger diameter big and little end bearings, new connecting rods to suit, and increased water-cooling flow around the engine.

Backing this were several other running gear improvements. There was a new type of hydrostatic clutch slave cylinder (which meant that free play was automatically taken up, and the 'bite' point in pedal travel did not move with time and wear), the Rapier III type of gearchange was adopted, wider rear leaf springs and larger lever-arm dampers were added, while new-type mud/dust shields were fitted to protect the front disc brakes. Someone had even found time to specify a three-ear petrol filler cap instead of the slippery round cap of the original car.

It was in the cockpit however (which meant 'in the showroom', where first impressions were so important) that the most obvious changes were made. Project engineer Alec Caine, a tall man with a passion for improving the Alpine, had spent much of the winter lobbying for improvements to the driving position – and got his way.

Not only were the seat slides relocated rearwards by two inches (51mm), but the pedal box was also pushed forward. There was a smaller diameter steering wheel (15in (381mm) instead of 16in (406mm)) which which was also mounted one inch (25mm) higher than before. The result was that Rootes claimed three inches (76mm) more leg room for tall drivers and a better driving position.

In theory the use of a three prong petrol filler cap is one way of identifying an Alpine II, compared with an Alpine I, but in later years many owners decided to do a bit of their own updating.

At Motor Shows Rootes liked to emphasize the links between the Alpine sports car and the Rapier sports saloon. This is the Geneva Motor Show of March 1961, with Alpines well to the fore.

Not only that, but there was now a chromed sliding guide ahead of the wind-up window glass, to eliminate any tendency to bow out at high speeds, along with extra features such as an optional map pocket and padded sun visors.

Rootes thought that all these improvements justified a price increase, though it was restricted to a mere £14. Most import-antly, at £986 what the Americans would call the 'sticker price' was still under the important psychological barrier of £1,000.

By calling up all the optional extras it was possible, however, to spend a lot more money than that, as this October 1960 list proves. I have converted into modern decimal currency, though left 1960 values alone!

Feature	Total Price
Sunbeam Alpine II	£985.71
Detachable hardtop	£ 60.00
Overdrive	£ 60.21
Centre-lock wire wheels	£ 38.25
Whitewall tyres	£ 8.15
Dunlop Road Speed tyres	£ 11.69
Road Speed whitewall tyres	£ 20.37
Tonneau cover	£ 10.00
Heater	£ 12.00
Radio	£ 22.05

A 'fully-loaded car' (a car fitted with all the options), therefore, could quite easily cost £1,200. Allowing for inflation, that would be about £14,000 in today's money. How does that stack up against your expectations? Rootes's advertising agents were nothing if not inventive, for their Alpine display ads of this period claimed that the Alpine was : 'Bred from success in the world's greatest rally events'. In that the Alpine's running gear was all developed from the Rapier, that was true, but at this point the factory had not yet pitted the Alpine itself against any major events – racing or rallying.

According to the artists who illustrated *The Autocar's* road tests, not all of that claimed 3.5 inches (88.9mm) was translated into extra leg room, though there was certainly more space behind the pedals, and below the steering wheel. The testers must have been somewhat nonplussed at first, for the latest car was no quicker than the original (as often happened in those days, there is a suspicion that the original press 'fleet' were in better-than-average condition).

Looking at the general behaviour, however, they wrote that:

undoubtedly it is now a two-seater of

special merit. ...The new power unit is smoother than before, particularly at low revs, and it is less obtrusive than before... [and finally:]... Designed and developed against a formidable background of experience and success in international rallies, the Sunbeam Alpine typifies a size and type of vehicle in which the British industry excels.

Lord Rootes, at least, must have been happy to see that *Road & Track* greeted the Alpine II with the comment:

Few of the cars coming to our shores are as obviously American-orientated as the products from England's Rootes Group, a company that manufactures a line of economy sedans that look for all the world as though their origin was Detroit, rather than Coventry. These cars reflect, if not exactly the average American's tastes, then at least what the Rootes people think they are... .

More than that, here was a magazine which reported a top speed of 100mph (160km/h) – most other journals found that their cars reached 97mph (155km/h) or 98mph (157km/h) at best – though the bad news was that testers carped about the door glass slide channel, which looked sharp and prickly when the glass was wound down away from it.

Harrington Alpines – Semi-Official 'Specials'

The original much-modified Harrington Alpine was introduced in March 1961, and although it was never built at a Rootes factory – neither at Armstrong-Siddeley's Parkside plant, nor at Ryton-on-Dunsmore – it was clear that there was a lot of Rootes support behind the project.

The South Coast based coachbuilders, Thomas Harrington, produced this very neat fastback conversion of the Alpine, marketing it (with Rootes's approval and help) as the Harrington Alpine...

...and identifying it with a smart Alpine-style badge on the boot lid.

It wasn't always easy to work out who owned who, or who influenced who, but those were the days in which Rootes also controlled the finances of several dealerships, of which the Robins & Day group was one. George Hartwell's Bournemouth based garage group might have been independent at the time, but Hartwell himself was a very close friend of the Rootes family, and became chairman of the Harrington concern too.

Whatever the financial dealing, all Harrington Alpines were produced in the same way. Every car started life as a standard machine that was then comprehensively modified into fastback hardtop types, with bodywork changes by Thomas Harrington, and tuned-up engines provided by George Hartwell Ltd. All but a handful were based on the 1.6-litre Alpine II types, complete with fins.

Type A : Although the conventional boot lid and the rear 'deck' was carved away, what became known (retrospectively) as the Type A Harrington retained almost all of the Alpine II's steel monocoque, on to which was grafted a moulded glass-fibre top. This fastback shape swept smoothly down to the tail, and embraced a small lift-up boot lid, but there is no doubt that artistically it did not sit completely comfortably with the very prominent fins.

Stiffness was assured by a multitude of connections along the screen rail, and there was an extra steel body crossmember across the car behind the sloping rear window, which was also an ideal place to hinge the boot lid. One bonus of the new all-in-one roof was that there was an extra two inches (51mm) of headroom in the cabin, a cabin which felt (and was) much more spa-

---

Harrington – the coachbuilding connection

Thomas Harrington, a wheelwright, founded his own coachbuilding company in Brighton in 1897. Thereafter the company grew steadily, remaining as a family business until 1963. Between the wars it concentrated on building coach bodies for Dennis, Bedford and Commer chassis, but in the 1920s Harrington also pioneered the use of the French Weymann method of construction for cars.

Along the way there was also time for Harrington to become UK concessionaires for various overseas marques, before also becoming a main dealer for Rootes cars.

Harrington moved to new premises at Old Shoreham Road, Hove, before the war, built many military vehicle bodies and airframes during the conflict, then reverted to producing bus, coach and commercial vehicles. Harrington became an important player in the 1950s with the launch of a major new project, a light-alloy, underfloor engined, chassisless coach, with running gear supplied by Commer (a Rootes subsidiary), and before long the legendary Rootes TS3 diesel engine also became an option.

Nevertheless, it was some years before Clifford Harrington (a grandson of the founder) led a team which got involved in the Harrington Alpine sports car project. A year after that car had appeared, Harrington also provided expertise for the Triumph TR4-based Dove GT model.

In the meantime, Harrington had been taken over by another Rootes main dealer (Robins & Day) which just so happened to be controlled by the Rootes family. Bournemouth Rootes dealer George Hartwell, a great friend of the Rootes family, became Harrington's chairman, and later Desmond Rootes took over the sales division. Incestuously, modified engines for these cars were supplied by George Hartwell Ltd.

By 1963 Harrington sales had dried up and the project folded. Apart from its presence on the frontage of a Rootes dealership on the South Coast, the Harrington name soon disappeared.

cious than the normal Alpine hardtop model.

Most of the luggage space was inside the car – behind the seats and above the line of the back axle, for when the boot lid was up, the opening revealed was dominated by the spare wheel and a floor above it. The luggage space was fully carpeted, and extra features included front-hinged rear quarter windows.

Normally a Harrington Alpine would be supplied with its engine in standard tune, but three different tuning stages were also available from George Hartwell Ltd, these ranging from a simple £25 kit (worth 88bhp, it was said) all the way up to a full-house racing £215 worth of FIA-approved kit for motorsport.

Two views of the interior of a Harrington Alpine, showing the very smart, up-market, brand of trimming, carpets and the use of a wooden dashboard. This car was photographed in the 1990s, which explains the use of saftey belts, because in the early 1960s virtually no one fitted them, and certainly did not use them.

Although the Harrington looked much heavier than standard, the makers claimed that the penalty was a mere 25lb (11kg). The financial penalty, on the other hand, was much higher. The original Harrington cost £1,225, which compared with £1,046 for a standard hardtop equipped Alpine. Most cars featured the newly-fashionable Microcell seats, though as each car was individually ordered there was a great deal of difference between individual machines.

From certain angles, particularly low down, the Harrington was a startling-looking car, and there was no doubt that it was a tighter-feeling ensemble than the original, but there was always the obstacle of the price. Was it worth paying an extra £179 – or 17 per cent – for the car? Thomas Harrington hoped that it was, and laid down a run of 100 cars.

Soon after it was launched, *Autosport*'s Editor, Gregor Grant, sampled a Stage III-tuned Harrington, which featured two side-draught twin-choke Weber carburet-tors, and for which 100bhp was claimed.

[Actually, a 20bhp – 25 per cent – improvement sounds very modest when the extent of the engine changes are concerned. Perhaps George Hartwell was being modest, over-cautious even.]

That particular car could reach 110mph (176km/h), accelerate from rest to 60mph (96km/h) in 10.6sec, and sprint the standing quarter-mile in 17.9sec, all of which was a lot better than the standard product.

Autocar tried a Stage II (93bhp at 5,700rpm) example which proved to be a lot slower than this, for it could not reach 100mph (160km/h), and took 12.7sec to reach 60mph (96km/h) from the traffic lights.

Harrington Le Mans (Type B): The next phase was for Harrington to change the style, and to capitalize on what had already been achieved at Le Mans by the 'works' Alpines in June 1961 – (see Chapter 9 for details).

The second generation Harrington-styled Alpine featured a new tail with cutback rear wings, and was known as the Harrington Le Mans. The proud owner of this car was H.R.H. Prince William of Gloucester.

In October 1961, therefore, a car called the Harrington Le Mans appeared (note that the name 'Alpine' had disappeared completely – for sale in the USA it was known as the Le Mans GT), this car not only having a modified fastback style, complete with lift-up hatchback (which must surely have been influenced by Jaguar's new E-Type Coupé?), with the rear fins cropped, all to help produce a waistline which swept down (rather than up) towards the rear.

The rear itself was different from the original Alpine, with a sharply cut-off panel holding a row of circular (stop, tail, and indicator) lights.

The adoption of a hatchback allowed the luggage area to be rejigged (once again, look at the E-Type Coupé to see where the inspiration came from), with a fold-down occasional rear seat allowing a 46inch (1,168mm) long platform, there was a different full-width facia trimmed in walnut, and by this time George Hartwell Ltd had settled on a 104bhp @ 6,000rpm engine tune.

Although Harrington, and Rootes, were keen to see this car sell in larger numbers (a minimum run of 1000 was envisaged), demand was always damped down by the high prices asked, and apparently only 250 were ever produced.

At launch the Harrington Le Mans retailed for £1,495, £415 more than the normal Alpine II hardtop of the day. Today, of course, this still sounds cheap, but after allowing for inflation, the mid-1990s ticket would be about £17,000.

Type C: One year after the Le Mans had been shown, Harrington tried again, this time with the Type C. By taking half a step back, and eliminating the expensive process of reshaping the steel rear wings, Harrington produced an interesting half-way house.

The latest and, as it transpired, the final production version therefore had the hard-top and lift-up hatchback feature of the (Type B) Le Mans, along with the standard rear fins, all married to a rather different rear tail cut off.

Costs, clearly, were well down, which explains the selling price of £1,196.64 in October 1962, still £178 more costly than the Alpine II hardtop, but much more reasonable it seemed.

However, the public seemed to have lost interest in these individualistic cars. Demand was right down, so when the Alpine II was replaced by the Alpine III early in 1963, serious production came to an end. Because there were subtle changes around the screen and glass of the Alpine III, more investment would have been needed to adopt the Harrington roof moulds, and in the end only a handful of Type Ds were ever produced.

Surprisingly, at least one other Harrington car was produced on the Alpine IV base, but this was definitely a one-off, and as far as is known there was no such thing as a Harrington Tiger. Total production of Harrington Alpines was between 400 and 450 – better than almost any other such project, but not good enough for Robins & Day to look on it as a long-term project.

Alpine Assembly Moves to Ryton: 1962

Early in 1962 the decision was made to wind-down the manufacture of Alpines at the Armstrong-Siddeley factory. Production at Parkside had always been subject to a contract of limited duration, but in happier times I suspect that Rootes would have been willing to extend the arrangement. Armstrong-Siddeley certainly would have been delighted, for it had stopped building Armstrong-Siddeley cars in mid-1960, and withdrawal of Alpines from the Burlington works would be a major blow.

These, though, were not happy times for Rootes. Not only was the company already committed to a colossal investment in a new factory at Linwood, near Glasgow (where Imps were to be built), but it had also just resisted a very damaging thirteen week strike at the British & Light Steel Pressings subsidiary in West London.

Rootes car production had plummeted from 149,290 in 1960 to a depressing 100,337 in 1961, with profits slumping alarmingly in the same period. Due to the BLSP strike, Rootes made a financial loss in 1961/1962 of £2 million – the most severe it had ever experienced.

To claw its way back into profit, therefore, Rootes had to rationalise and concentrate its business wherever possible. As one of several measures (dropping the Minx and Gazelle convertibles was another) it decided to bring Alpine assembly back into Ryton.

As the city's local paper, the *Coventry Evening Telegraph*, stated on 23 March 1962 :

Production of Sunbeam Alpine sports cars at the Coventry factory of Bristol Siddeley

Engines [the official name for the Armstrong-Siddeley business in Coventry, which was now part of a larger industrial complex] came to an end today... Bristol Siddeley have now fulfilled the terms of the original contract and the car division has been closed...

As part of Rootes's new strategy, all the assembly facilities for Alpine monocoques (framing and welding had previously been at Parkside) were centred at the Pressed Steel factory in Cowley, where PS Co also painted and trimmed the shells. These were then trucked to Ryton, where the cars were completed on a dedicated assembly line.

There was a short overlap while Alpines were being built in both factories. For Armstrong-Siddeley, the downside was that 350 assembly workers had to be sacked, though a number of these moved smoothly up to Ryton to carry on building Alpines.

In the meantime, Rootes designers and development engineers had been as active as ever. Not only had a new range of family cars – Hillman Super Minx, Singer Vogue and Humber Sceptre – been developed, but the Alpine itself had been steadily improved. It was time to introduce a further version – the Alpine III.

4 Alpine III and IV – Up-Market Sports Cars

Anyone working in the Rootes Group in the 1960s could be certain of one thing: there was never a dull moment. Lord Rootes and his planners never seemed to want to let a good product settle down. Even if it was selling well, there would always be some new gimmick, some styling or technical tweak, or some modification which just *had* to be included.

All of which explains why there would be so much change in such a short time, and why the Alpine Series V appeared only six years after the original car went on sale. (In the same period, Triumph introduced two new TR sports cars, and MG only one).

Not that there was anything new about this Rootes itch to improve. Post-war, for instance, there had already been seven Marks of monocoque Minx in nine years, seven versions of post-war Humber Hawk and six derivatives of the postwar Sunbeam–Talbot range. There wasn't a year when Billy Rootes didn't come back from one or other of the big shows, his mind full of an innovation he had seen on a rival product, and demand that it be included in his own models within the year!

The record shows that the Alpine II was unveiled in October 1960, and that the Alpine III did not appear until March 1963. By Rootes standards this was an extraordinarily long time between model changes, or facelifts, but in this case there were many good reasons why should it have been so.

In this period not only were the engineers bound up with the design of the launch of the Hillman Super Minx/Singer Vogue/Humber Sceptre generation of saloons, but there was a mountain of work to be done on the layout of the all-new rear-engined Hillman Imp.

That, and the need to relocate Alpine assembly from the Armstrong-Siddeley factory at Parkside to the main Rootes plant at Ryton-on-Dunsmore, meant that the Alpine II was left to make its own reputation for thirty months.

Work on improvements to the Alpine II, however, had begun even before that car had gone on sale, and it all stemmed from a visit which project engineer Alec Caine had made to Carrozzeria Touring of Milan in 1959. Not only was this Italian coachbuilding company interested in taking up a local-assembly agreement for the Alpine, but it also wanted to develop a new model entirely: that would be the Sunbeam Venezia, which made its debut in 1963.

Touring, at the time a successful, not to say cocky, Italian coachbuilding house, was convinced that it could improve the Alpine, and said so. At first there was little enthusiasm in Coventry for this approach, as Rootes was still well dug in to its 'Britain is always best' attitude to design.

Once he had established commercial links with Touring, however, Lord Rootes

Carrozzeria Touring of Milan – Italian styling excellence

Founded in Italy in 1925, Touring was one of a resourceful new breed of independent Italian coach-builders which first of all built special car bodies to order, then began to co-operate more and more with Italian and other manufacturers.

In the 1950s the company developed a new type of body construction, where body styles were built up on a framework of small-diameter tubes clothed in aluminium, this method becoming known as the 'Superleggera' (which is the Italian word for 'super lightweight').

As far as British car enthusiasts were concerned, Touring became famous in 1958, not only for being credited with the styling of the new Aston Martin DB4, but because that car's body shell also used 'Superleggera' principles.

The Rootes introduction to Touring (and the arrangement for Touring to start building Alpines for sale in Europe) is described in the main text. However, Touring also developed a smart 2+2 Coupé model on the basis of the Humber Sceptre's body platform and all running gear.

This new car, called the Sunbeam Venezia, had a coupé style which naturally used Superleggera principles, along with a Sceptre windscreen, a Rapier grille, and Alpine tail lamps! Commercially this car was a failure, for only 145 such cars were produced from 1963 to 1965.

Carrozzeria Touring hit final trouble in 1965, and was officially wound up at that point, but such were the vagaries of Italian law that Touring still had time to complete the approved style for the new Jensen Interceptor of 1966 before the doors finally closed in 1967.

agreed that a development Alpine should be delivered to Italy to allow Touring to make a series of changes. Principally these would concentrate on the boot area, where there was a serious lack of stowage capacity on existing models, and on the fixtures and fittings in and around the cabin.

Touring's proposal was practical, and effective, but it meant making changes to the body platform. Basically, Touring proposed to relocate the spare wheel, by mounting it vertically on the forward wall of the boot area (behind the occasional seat and the soft-top stowage area, in other words), to ditch the original fuel tank, and replace it by two new tanks, one each to be tucked into the sides of the boot under the rear fins.

Since the floor was based on the Hillman Husky (even though this had been modified with the addition of the cruciform bracing under the floor) there was resistance to this from the planners unless the wheel could be mounted above the main pressing, for they did not relish having to 'sell' the

cost of making new press tools to the Rootes family. Since the time had now come to ditch the Husky completely, however, it meant that the Alpine's platform could develop on its own – which was an ideal excuse for specifying telescopic dampers for the first time !

Touring's own installation on the prototype was crudely engineered, but it gave Rootes the general idea, and would be more elegantly carried out in the coming months. It was, however, only one of a whole series of changes and improvements which would make up the Alpine III 'package'.

At a casual glance, there was one obvious visual difference between the Alpine II of 1960 and the Alpine III – there was now a small, triangular-shaped fixed quarterlight atop the doors, which mated to the windscreen pillars when the doors were closed. Qualms over safety had finally convinced Rootes that the freestanding channel 'spike' of the Alpine II was not desirable – and, in any case, a quarter window would provide that important bit of extra protection from draughts. In addition, the original rounded hardtop option was discarded, to be replaced by a more angular hardtop, which had more glass and altogether more elegant lines.

But that was only the start of it. Engines were little changed (but there would be two different tunes – to be described later), and the chassis was left alone, but there were major (Touring-inspired) changes in the boot, there was a sophisticated new adjustable steering column, and a much more comfortable interior which included reclinable front seats.

THE ALPINE III PACKAGE – TRIM AND FURNISHINGS

The most important marketing move was to split the Alpine into two slightly different models – Sports Tourer and GT. If you bought a Sports Tourer (for £840 in March 1963) the new-style hardtop was still available as an optional extra. If, on the other hand, you specified an Alpine GT, this came complete with hardtop, but although you could remove this as usual, there was no fold-back soft-top as part of the specification.

Sports Tourers had a slightly more powerful version of the 1.6-litre engine than before – it was rated at 82bhp instead of 80 bhp (both figures being net) – this improvement being found by fitting slightly larger inlet valves.

The Alpine GT, on the other hand, was fitted with an engine which had been re-equipped to make it less noisy, with carburettor air being fed through a micro-element air cleaner, then through flexible trunking, and with a single-outlet cast iron exhaust manifold instead of the more familiar tubular manifold. This resulted in 77bhp (net) at 5,000rpm, with a slight loss of peak torque.

At the same time the layout of the cooling system was changed. The original cast alloy header tank had been abandoned, there now being a vertical flow radiator with an integral top tank.

To produce the Alpine III from the Alpine II, apart from the fuel filler cap (still on the right side, which was inconvenient for UK customers, but exactly right for USA drivers) being moved up towards the peak of the rear wing, there were virtually no changes to the exterior style of the open-topped car.

When the optional hardtop was fitted, however, there was no doubt about this being a new car. The new hardtop was an altogether more substantial unit (for which, read 'heavier'). Instead of a wrap-round rear window, which had always aped the line of the Rapier's rear window shape, there was now a larger, more rectangular, and almost flat pane, with neat triangular-shaped glass behind the doors themselves: these could be swung slightly open to increase through-flow ventilation.

If you looked carefully, too, you would also find new-type shields on each front wing, under the 'Alpine' script, which succinctly mentioned 'SIII'.

Rootes, its engineers in particular, were still exercised with thoughts of improving the Alpine's driving position, its versatility, with a great deal of work going into providing new seats, a new steering column, and adjustable pedals.

At this point I should remind those who do not know, *all* the major Rootes engineering personalities of the day with Alpine influence – Peter Ware, Peter Wilson and Alec Caine – were tall and thin, which explains why there was such emphasis on this work. Lord Rootes, on the other hand, was quite stout, but of medium height, while his son Geoffrey was also a rather small, dapper, man. It was easy to see, therefore, that to keep all the bosses happy, an Alpine had to be almost infinitely adjustable !

The most obvious improvement was to the seats, that not only looked better than before, and could be reclined all the way until they made contact with the rear cross-member or bulkhead, but were also more comfortable than earlier types.

Legend has it that Rootes designers were led to a Surrey-based company, Microcell Ltd, by a chance conversation between Peter Ware and Sir George Edwards of British Aerospace, who apparently stated that : 'there is only one group of people who know anything about designing seats suitable for long-distance travelling, and they are the aircraft seat manufacturers'.

That may be so, but as an active rally co-driver of the day, I can also note that the rallying business (which included the Rootes 'works' team) had already discovered Microcell seats, and were already using them in 'works' Rapiers and Alpines. Not only that, but Microcell supplied seating to Thomas Harrington Ltd., for use in the Harrington Alpines.

The Microcell-style seats chosen for the Alpine III were rather different from those used by rally teams, not least in that they were less wrapround at hip level. Apart from looking good, and feeling comfortable, there was also the possibility of separate height adjustment at front and rear, while the backrest angle could be changed through a very wide arc.

As in recent Alpines, there was also a fore-and-after adjustment of 1.6in (40mm) for the brake and clutch pedals, all of which meant that it was now possible to cater for tall men (pedals forward, seat right back, seat down close to the floorpan) or for small women (pedals back, seat forward, seat at the top of its adjustment).

Not only that, but Rootes also provided a steering column which was adjustable for length. By loosening off a knurled locking collar in the centre of the wheel, the wheel could be withdrawn from the column shroud by up to three inches (76mm). This was the feature, incidentally, which could occasionally go wrong, and if the collar failed to lock, the wheel could float disconcertingly up and down. Although there was no likelihood of the wheel coming adrift completely, it felt like it – very worrying.

Compared with the Alpine II, the entire interior of the latest car looked more inviting. The facia of the Sports Tourer had a black crackle finish, while that of the GT was a polished wood slab. The passenger now got a grab handle ahead of him (few people wore safety belts in those days, don't forget, even when they were fitted), and there were revisions to the switch gear. This time, too, there were two-speed windscreen wipers and a windscreen washer. The Tourer retained its plastic covered steering wheel, but the GT got a wooden wheel rim.

Better yet, the so-called 'occasional' seat looked more welcoming than before, as the cushion and the side and rear panels all now had ribbing to break up the previous slabs of plain plastic cloth. Amazingly, although there was now a lockable glove box between the front seats, which doubled as an arm rest, there was virtually no other stowage, not even slim pockets in the doors such as offered by the Alpine's rivals.

The major repackaging job had been concentrated in the boot area, where Rootes had studied Touring's proposals, refined them quite a lot, and taken account of the next change, which would lead to the launch of the Alpine IV in 1964.

The original layout of the Alpine I/Alpine

II, with a horizontal spare wheel, and with the nine Imperial gallon fuel tank (of Husky type) underneath it, had been abandoned. In its place, the false floor to the very shallow boot had been discarded, and the 5.90-13in. spare wheel/tyre had been repositioned, vertically-mounted, at the front-end of what suddenly became a much deeper boot.

Twin fuel tanks were specified, each fitted inside the shape of the rear wings, interconnected by piping, and with a single filler cap on the right – the capacity going up to 11.25 Imperial gallons. Maybe that doesn't sound much of an improvement, but in fact it enlarged fuel capacity by one quarter, and stretched the useable fuel range accordingly.

Chassis Improvements – Detail Development Again

There is a great difference between what engineers would like to do, and what can be afforded. Peter Wilson once told the author that he would have liked to see the entire suspension redeveloped to provide a firmer ride, and he would certainly have liked to provide the heavy rear beam axle with more positive location, but that none of this could ever be afforded.

For the Alpine III, therefore, the team had to be satisfied with using a reinforced cross-member (this was sturdy enough for the Alpine, in all truth, but changes were once again being made across the range), with specifying a larger diameter front anti-roll bar, and with using telescopic rear dampers of Rapier type instead of the original lever-arm dampers.

Incidentally, to show that such changes were never tackled lightly, let me remind you that to change from lever-arm to telescopic dampers also involved specifying different axle fixings and – much more impor-

tant – it meant making considerable changes to the body/chassis platform in that area. It all took time, it all took testing and it all cost a great deal of money.

The last significant chassis change was to specify larger-diameter front brake discs (now they were 9.85in (250mm) in diameter), and to specify a brake vacuum servo as standard. That, at least, put a stop to the earlier complaints that the brakes were too heavy, especially for lady drivers who made a significant proportion of the Alpine's clientele.

ALPINE III ON THE MARKET

As I noted at the head of this chapter, no sooner had Rootes revealed a new model than they started making changes to it. Only four months after the Alpine III had been revealed, therefore, the company made a major change to the engine specification – ditching the twin downdraught Zenith carburettors and their related manifolds, in favour of a new Solex 'Compound' carburettor (for which read, dual choke with progressive choke opening).

The same change was made at the same time to other Rootes cars using the aluminium cylinder head/sporty tune version of the 1.6-litre engine, notably the Humber Sceptre (which was badged as a Sunbeam Rapier in styling pictures taken only months before its launch!), and the Sunbeam Rapier.

Declared as being for the improvement of fuel economy, there is no doubt that this change was also made to reduce costs. Certainly it could have done nothing for the engine's performance, as a brief look at the angularities of the inlet manifold proved.

Testers surveying the Alpine III could not have known that yet another derivative,

The facelifted Alpine III was unveiled in the spring of 1963, but would only have a ten month life. This was an exciting launch-time display. By the looks of the parquet floor, I believe this was mounted on the ground floor of Devonshire House, in London. Note the much changed lines of the hardtop, and the immaculate sectioned engine/gearbox in front of it. A pity Rootes publicists couldn't spell 'Turismo'.

the Alpine IV, would appear only ten months later : what could Rootes have been thinking of? Faced with the impression that most improvements had concentrated on equipment and furnishings, rather than on performance, most of them tried to get to grips with the idea of a rather 'softer' Alpine GT.

Autocar, who tested the Alpine GT in September 1963 – only four months before it would, in any case, be dropped after a short life – recorded a top speed of 98mph (157km/h) for the Solex 'Compound' equipped car, which was becoming almost traditional for this car. Because the GT had more sound-deadening material fitted to

reduce noise, and because the new hardtop was more solid than before, the Alpine GT was heavier than before, and accelerated slightly slower – taking 14.9 seconds to reach 60mph (96km/h) from rest.

General impressions were that there had been real improvements wherever the chassis had been changed – the testers noting lighter steering, better roadholding, and a much lighter pedal pressure for the brakes. Pointing out that the rearranged fuel tankage had virtually doubled the stowage space, they also reported an improved average fuel range of about 270 miles (432km), much better than before.

For the Alpine III, the biggest improvement was hidden away – in the boot. The spare wheel was relocated, and positioned vertically at the front of the boot, while twin fuel tanks were fitted (tucked into each wing). This made the boot much more spacious than before, and the Alpine much more versatile.

The Grand Touring version, [they summarized] is a sophisticated form of transport...The attention which has been paid to the seating will be specially appreciated on very long journeys. What the car may lack in punch it makes up for in the relative quietness of its progress: and one must admire its good looks.

Road & Track felt much the same way, commenting that:

This is a car intended to be comfortable for everyone from the Cardiff Giant to J.Fred Muggs. [In addition] The Alpine's ride and handling are exceptional. The car will glide along as smoothly as a 2-ton sedan, and yet does not bob or sway. When pressed, the Alpine's springing seems to stiffen, and it suddenly turns into a pure sporting machine.

Series III Alpines had a better trimmed rear compartment than before, but (especially with the hardtop fitted) this was still no better than a useful stowage area.

Even so, the sports car world did not seem to be quite as impressed by the Alpine III as Rootes hoped. The production figures show that 5,863 cars were produced in ten months, an average of about 150 Alpines a week, which was not nearly as many as MG was producing MGBs, or Triumph was producing TR4s.

Although we do not know what proportion of those cars were Alpine GTs, we do know that many prospective buyers shied away from paying more for a car that was slower, and somehow less sporty, than earlier Alpines. In vain did Rootes point out

Alpine III (1963 – 1964)

Numbers Built
5,863

Layout
Unit-construction body/chassis structure, with steel panels. Two-door, front engine/rear drive, sold as two-seater open sports car, with optional steel hardtop. GT model available only in Hardtop form

Engine

Type	Rootes
Block material	Cast iron
Head material	Cast aluminium
Cylinders	4 in-line
Cooling	Water
Bore and stroke	81.5 × 76.2mm
Capacity	1,592cc
Main bearings	3
Valves	2 per cylinder, operated by in-line overhead valves, pushrods and rockers, with camshaft mounted in block, driven by chain from crankshaft.
Compression ratio	9.1:1
Carburettors	2 Zenith 36 WIP3
Max. power	(Tourer) 82bhp (net) @ 5,200rpm (GT) 77bhp (net) at 5,000rpm
Max. torque	(Tourer) 94 @ 3,800rpm (GT) 91 @ 3,500rpm lb/ft

Transmission
Four-speed manual gearbox, with synchromesh on top, third and second gears. Optional Laycock overdrive on top and third gears

Clutch	Single dry plate; hydraulically operated

Overall gearbox ratios

Top	3.89
3rd	4.80
2nd	7.38
1st	11.53
Reverse	14.61
Final drive	3.89:1

Overdrive (Laycock) was optional, on top and third gears, with the same 3.89:1 final drive ratio. Overall 'overdrive' ratios were:

Top (O/D)	3.12
3rd (O/D)	3.85

Suspension and steering

Front	Independent, coil springs, wishbones, anti-roll bar, telescopic dampers
Rear	Live (beam) axle, by half-elliptic leaf springs, telescopic dampers
Steering	Recirculating ball

Tyres	5.90-13in cross-ply
Wheels	Steel disc, bolt-on, or optional centre-lock wire spoke
Rim width	4.0in

Brakes

| Type | Disc brakes at front, drums at rear, hydraulically operated |
| Size | 9.85in diameter front discs, 9 × 1.75in rear drums |

Dimensions (in/mm)

Track	
Front	51/1295
Rear	48.5/1232
Wheelbase	86/2184
Overall length	155.25/3943
Overall width	60.5/1537m
Overall height	(Tourer) 51.5/1308, (GT) 52.5/1334
Unladen weight	2,220lb/1,007kg

Alpine IIIs and Sunbeam Rapier IVs together on the Sunbeam stand at the Earls Court Motor Show in October 1963.

that the GT was a better Alpine than before, better handling, better equipped, and better behaved. The 'wottle' merchants ('What'll she do, mister?') still wanted more performance, and would seemingly put up with a lot to achieve that.

Alpine IV – So Soon?

Almost everyone was astonished to see the Alpine III dropped after only ten months, to be replaced by the rather different Alpine IV. Even by Rootes's frenetic standards, this was taking the quest for regular change a bit far.

It now seems that the changes ushered in to produce the Alpine IV had already been on the boil well before the Alpine III was launched, but that it was not considered wise to delay the launch of a new type (Alpine III, that is) until all could be made available as a package.

From the three-quarter tail view, the Alpine IV looked smarter than the Series III, for the new smaller rear fins were a better match for the angular hardtop style.

On Alpine III, IV and V types, the optional hardtop was a more angular style than the original, with more glass area.

Alpine IV (1964 – 1965)

Numbers Built
12,406

Layout
Unit-construction body/chassis structure, with steel panels. Two-door, front engine/rear drive, sold as two-seater open sports car, with optional steel hardtop.

Engine

Type	Rootes
Block material	Cast iron
Head material	Cast aluminium
Cylinders	4 in-line
Cooling	Water
Bore and stroke	81.5 × 76.2mm
Capacity	1,592cc
Main bearings	3
Valves	2 per cylinder, operated by in-line overhead valves, pushrods and rockers, with camshaft mounted in block, driven by chain from crankshaft
Compression ratio	9.2:1
Carburettors	1 Solex Compound 32 PAIA
Max. power	80.5bhp (net) @ 5,000rpm
Max. torque	93lb/ft @ 3,500rpm

Transmission
Four-speed manual gearbox, with synchromesh on top, third and second gears at first: all-synchromesh from autumn 1964. Optional Laycock overdrive on top and third gears.

Clutch	Single dry plate; hydraulically operated

Overall gearbox ratios

Top	3.89
3rd	5.41
2nd	8.32
1st	13.01
Reverse	16.48
Final drive	3.89:1

Overdrive (Laycock) was optional, on top and third gears, when the final drive ratio became 4.22:1. Overall transmission ratios were:

Top (O/D)	3.39
Top (direct)	4.22
3rd (O/D)	4.72
3rd (direct)	5.87
2nd	9.04
1st	14.13
Reverse	17.90
Final drive	4.22

Borg Warner Type 35 automatic transmission was also optional on this Alpine model only.

Overall automatic gearbox ratios

Direct drive	3.89
Intermediate range	5.64
Low range	9.31
Reverse	8.14
Final drive	3.89

Suspension and steering

Front	Independent, coil springs, wishbones, anti-roll bar, telescopic dampers
Rear	Live (beam) axle, by half-elliptic leaf springs, telescopic dampers
Steering	Recirculating ball
Tyres	5.90-13in cross-ply
Wheels	Steel disc, bolt-on, or optional centre-lock wire spoke
Rim width	4.5in

Brakes

Type	Disc brakes at front, drums at rear, hydraulically operated
Size	9.85in diameter front discs, 9×1.75in rear drums

Dimensions (in/mm)

Track	
Front	51/1295
Rear	48.5/1232
Wheelbase	86/2184
Overall length	156/3962
Overall width	60.5/1537
Overall height	51.5/1308
Unladen weight	2,220lb/1,007kg

This time round, Rootes not only made further changes to the Alpine's running gear (automatic transmission became optional for the first time), but for the first and only time the stylists had also been allowed to make changes to the shape of the car. Along with further improvements to the interior, this was yet another appealing package, which would have a life of about twenty months.

This time round, the rear end of the car had been reshaped, just in time for the same style to be applied to the new Tiger (see Chapter 5), and for the same smart new tail lamp clusters to be used on the Italian-built Sunbeam Venezia sports coupé.

Simply put, this involved cropping the fins, producing a more subtle (and rounded) rear quarter shape. Kenneth Howes, who had styled the original Alpine, was long gone, while the United States fashion for exaggerated fins was also in decline. This, and the fact that Touring had shown its own version of cropped fins when producing the vertical spare wheel/twin petrol tank package of 1961, inspired Lord Rootes to approve the change.

Roy Axe, by then rising through the ranks of the Rootes styling department, is clear about the influences:

Everything progressed relatively quietly with the exception of toning down the fins, which everyone was doing, and therefore the Alpine had to follow suit.

I'm sure that, eventually, this was a Rootes family decision. I'm quite sure the elimination of the fins came after Billy Rootes had been to a show, found all the fins being turned down, and decided he had to follow.

No new car proposals for all-new Alpines, to my recollection – and I was there throughout that time – were ever really done. There were all kinds of tweaks and improvements – grille changes and so on – proposed, but these were all very minor.

The proposed changes really came about with the Tiger and the advent of Chrysler...

As before, it was body engineer Dick Newman who had the responsibility of turning the agreed styling changes into reality, and pushing the drawings out to Pressed Steel for action. As someone who was in and around the motor industry at that time, I know that the Lucas tail lamps would already have been settled (even before the rear wing shape was finalized)

The Alpine IV had its rear wings and fins trimmed down for styling reasons, though this did not cause any reduction in boot space. As before, there were two fuel tanks.

Dating from 1962/1963, these were the two clay styles considered for use in the Alpine IV. As you can see, only one car was used for these experiments, with the more complex proposal (which included what look like Hillman Imp tail/indicator lamps) rejected in favour of a simpler pressing.

because it seemed to take ages for Lucas to prepare plastic lens mouldings in those days.

Although there were new wing pressings – rear quarter panels, really – that was the only 'sheet metal' alteration between Alpine III and Alpine IV. At the same time, yet another type of fuel filler cap – this being a flush-fitting, lockable, type – was specified, but all the internal panels, the boot area, and the still-new twin fuel tank arrangement of the Alpine III were retained.

At the front, the 'Sunbeam' bonnet badge had disappeared, being replaced by another badge inside the single cross-bar of the new front grille. There were amber turn indicators at the front, rubber-faced bumper over-riders, and 'SIV' shields on the front wings and the tail.

The engine development engineers, and the product planners, had produced yet more new ideas. The lower-powered Alpine GT (III) package had clearly not worked, so this was dumped, the Alpine reverted to a single power output for both models – yet at the same time, the engine was quieter than before.

Once again there was only a simple micronic air cleaner atop the Solex 'Compound' carburettor, and the crankcase breathing system was now self-consuming, but this time round there was yet another exhaust manifold – a cast iron item which replicated the old tubular manifold.

The result was a claimed output of 82bhp at 5,200rpm – the same as with the higher-powered derivative of the Alpine III. As before, the IV's top speed was around 98mph (157km/h) – and I now believe this was because the Alpine's style, pretty though it was, had a rather poor aerodynamic shape.

Rootes had no wind tunnel of its own, and little desire, it seemed, to learn anything from one. As far as I know, after its original sessions at MIRA when the car was being shaped in 1956, the Alpine was never returned to that tunnel, and we do not know what the Alpine's drag coefficient (Cd) actually was.

How much faster, for instance, would the Alpine have been without those headlamp

Over the years the Rootes 'shield' surrounded a whole variety of lettering and information. In this case (as also used in the appropriate Rapier), this indicated the Series IV (not the Series 4, please note) Alpine.

From the start up of Alpine IV assembly, January 1964, there was a smart new side lamp/indicator cluster, and a simplified grille, plus rubber-faced overriders, but the headlamp hoods were retained.

hoods, without those prominent front wings, and with a smaller and more carefully-detailed front grille?

This was the moment, too, when Rootes's marketing staff fell into the same trap as several other European manufacturers. Because the Americans loved automatic transmission in their own domestic cars, the reasoning went, they would surely queue up to buy European sports cars with the same feature.

Wrong then, and wrong later, they didn't seem to realise that Americans bought European sports cars with a 'stick shift' precisely because of what they were. There was the tradition that you had to row a small (by American standards) European car along by changing gear frequently.

There was also the well-founded suspicion that cars like the Alpine simply didn't have sufficient spare torque to deal with the power losses inherent in fluid-coupling transmissions, and still retain acceptable performance.

No matter. Rootes engineers, having matched the new British-made Borg

Rootes was proud of its restyled Alpine IV, so in January 1964 it issued this plain side-view study with the press pack. On this car, however, both the white-wall tyres and the centre-lock wire spoke wheels were optional extras.

Warner Type 35 three-speed automatic to other cars in their medium-size range (but, significantly enough, not the Rapier), repeated the trick for the Alpine, equipping the Alpine IV with a quadrant selector which was placed on the tunnel in the same position as the normal gear lever.

Once again there was a change of heart over final drive ratios. On the Alpine III, the same 3.89:1 axle had been used, whether an overdrive was fitted or not and, predictably enough, this led to complaints that the overall gearing 'in overdrive' was much too high. Accordingly, for the Alpine IV, there were two different ratios once again – 4.22:1 being specified for overdrive cars, just as it had been for Alpine I and Alpine II types !

[Just in case you think that Peter Ware's experienced engineers should have known better, let me remind you that under Harry Webster and Spen King, Triumph made exactly the same mistake, at one point, with the GT6 Coupé - starting right, later modifying the ratios and getting the wrong result, then finally getting it right again before the end.]

Everyone, it seems, was happy to see the Alpine improving so steadily as its career progressed, and there wasn't a bad word written about the new finless rear style. The automatic transmission option (an extra £90.72, on top of the tax-paid price of £852.44) was much more controversial, most testers damning it with faint praise.

Motor's test of an automatic transmission car, in October 1964, emphasized the advantages and the drawbacks. While testers thought it was a 'pleasant tourer for two', there's no doubt that the reduced top speed (92mph), (147km/h) and the reduced acceleration (0–60mph in 18 seconds) was a disappointment. This was the slowest Alpine yet, by a significant margin and no amount of easy-to-drive automatic transmission ability could make up for that.

To quote *Motor*: 'The Alpine does not go as fast as its rakish looks might suggest.... but for comfortable driving in elegant surroundings it has few peers among

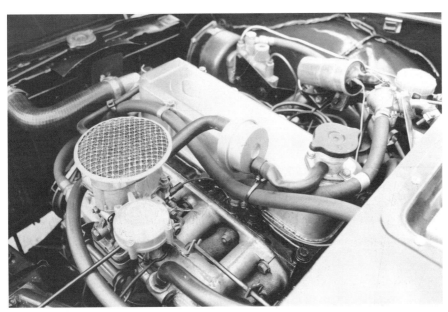

During the life of the Alpines, the twin downdraught carburettor installation was abandoned in favour of this single, downdraught dual choke ('compound') Solex instrument: according to the figures issued by Rootes, there was no effect on power and torque figures.

This is a very rare example of a Harrington conversion being carried out on the Alpine IV shell, complete with reduced size rear fins, for series production of Harrington Alpines had ended in 1963.

mass-production two-seaters.'

Incidentally, in case you think *Motor's* car was slightly down on power, I see that *Road & Track's* similar car was slightly quicker through the gears, but could only reach 90mph (144km/h) flat out.

The fact of the matter is that the automatic transmission option was a failure, but this didn't harm the Alpine IV in general. A good car (Alpine III) had been made even better (Alpine IV), and the Ryton assembly lines continued to churn out thirty or forty cars a day.

All-Synchromesh for 1965

At the Motor Show in October 1964, Rootes introduced a new design of all-synchromesh gearbox, which it standardized on every car in the medium-sized category – Hillman Minx and Super Minx, Singer Gazelle and Vogue, Humber Sceptre, Sunbeam Rapier and Alpine.

Although there was nothing wrong with the old box which was made obsolete, the 'all-synchromesh' move was a marketing imperative. Quite simply, if Ford (with the Cortina/Corsair), Vauxhall (with the Victor) and Triumph (with the 2000/TR4) had opted for all-synchromesh, then Rootes simply had to follow suit.

The old gearbox had featured synchromesh on top, third and second gears, and the design was in any case much modified from the original type, which had been laid out with a steering column gearshift in mind. The new box had synchromesh on all forward gears, and was really a very clever modification of the old (with no changes to most of the gear ratios, the gearwheels and components) but had a casing and selectors laid out for a centre floor, or remote-control central, gear lever position.

For the Alpine, here is a comparison of the internal ratios of the old, and the new, gearboxes:

Gearbox	Internal ratios
Old-type, no synchromesh on first gear	(Overdrive 0.803), Top 1.00, 3rd 1.392, 2nd 2.141, 1st 3.346, reverse 4.239:1
New-type, with synchromesh on all forward gears	(Overdrive 0.803), Top 1.00, 3rd 1.392, 2nd 2.141, 1st 3.353, reverse 3.569:1

Two studies of a close relative to the Alpine, the Sunbeam Venezia, which was built in small numbers by Carrozzeria Touring of Italy in the early 1960s. The Venezia used broadly similar engine and transmissions as the Alpine, but was based on the longer and rather different platform of the Humber Sceptre, and was a four-seater.

As can be seen, there was very little change between the old and the new boxes. The large first gear wheel towards the back of the box had been recessed to take the synchromesh cone, while reverse gear now drove through the third gear ratio towards the front of the box.

This meant that there was a different gearchange pattern. On all earlier Alpines, reverse had been found by pushing the lever to the left and back (alongside second gear). Now, with the new arrangement, reverse was to the right and back (alongside the top gear slot). For those who worried about such things, this made a quick change from first to reverse that much more difficult.

For 1965, therefore, the Alpine was a better car, and more competitive, than it had ever been. Still not quite capable of 100mph (160km/h) in a straight line, it now had the best transmission in the business, certainly the best-equipped interior, and there were many people who also thought that it was the best-looking of the British sports car crop.

If only Rootes management had not been totally bound up with the momentous decision to link up with Chrysler, with the continuing battle to make sense of the new Imp project in the Linwood factory in Scotland, and with the intensive programme to get a new-generation medium-sized family car (the Hillman Hunter – 'Arrow' – range), there might have been more time to spend on the Alpine project.

Not even the Ware/Wilson engineering axis had much spare time, either, as the Tiger (see Chapter 5) had just gone on sale, and because of all the Ford-versus-Chrysler V8 engine implications this car was taking up a disproportionate amount of their time.

At this moment, therefore, I hope I can spend a little time in 'if only' mode. If only the Alpine had been a genuine 100mph (160km/h) car (perhaps with a larger engine, more power and/or better aerodynamics) it might have sold better. If only Rootes's new partners, Chrysler, had tried harder to move Alpines through their showrooms in North America, If only...

Yet, even as it was, the Alpine IV was the class of the field in so many ways. Few argued with its styling, which was generally agreed to be more elegant than most. No-one argued with its refinement, its fittings, or its equipment, which were probably the Best of British. It was reliable, simple to maintain, comfortable to drive – and all it needed was a bit more pizzazz.

That, Rootes decided, could be provided for in 1966. For the Alpine V, a larger and more powerful engine was on the way.

5 Tiger – Born in the USA

When you consider just a few of the names behind the development of the V8 engined Tiger, it's easy to see why it was such a sports car of character. Not only was Carroll Shelby involved, but double F1 World Champion Jack Brabham had an input. American racing driver Ken Miles got his hands dirty around the project, Ian Garrad (son of Norman) was a guiding light, while Ford USA provided the basic hardware.

At this point it's important to stress that the Tiger was a brave new model conceived in a hurry, developed in a hurry, and put on sale well before it could reasonably have been expected to be ready. This was extra-ordinary because then, as later, Rootes was renowned for developing new models at a certain pace, and for not putting them into the showrooms before all the bugs were wrung out - but not with the Tiger !

Looking back from the 1990s, when we are used to seeing cars taking four or even more years to get from the 'Good Idea' state to public launch, it takes some believing to note that the Tiger project achieved that goal in just fourteen *months*. Specifically, it was Ian Garrad and Brian Rootes who first discussed the idea of a 'Thunderbolt' (for that was its original name) in February 1963, while the Tiger first met its public at the New York Show in April 1964, and production actually started at the end of June 1964.

The name 'Tiger' was chosen so late that there was only just time to apply the name to the car which appeared in New York,

which also carried a '260' shield on its flanks and tail.

Furthermore, the first Shelby-built car didn't even run until the end of April 1963, and didn't arrive back in the UK until July. Nine months later it was introduced, as a production car, and within a year it was being produced in numbers. Today that sort of schedule would be unthinkable, and even then it was quite unprecedented. Not even the Austin-Healey 100 of 1952–1953 had made it from the 'Good Idea' state to production as quickly.

Of course there were earlier influences to encourage the development of a high-performance version of the Alpine, though nothing was done to follow these up. It all started in the early 1960s, when the Alpine was still struggling to build a reputation in the USA. 'Works' race cars had been entered in high-profile sporting events (see Chapter 9), where they had been reliable and impressive, but the fact was that they were not as fast as some of their more established rivals.

Then, in 1962, the retired American racing driver (and 1959 Le Mans winner in a 'works' Aston Martin DBR1) Carroll Shelby's bright idea of mating the latest Ford V8 engine with the ageing AC Ace structure had seen the birth of the AC Cobra. Within months, every enthusiasts' motoring magazine in the USA was raving about the Cobra, and even though it was only selling in very limited numbers, it had set every other manufacturer to think about *their* future.

Shelby, Ford, and Ford V8 engines

Born in the USA in 1923, Carroll Shelby did not start racing until he was twenty-nine years old, and first joined the Aston Martin 'works' team in 1954. By the late 1950s he was a fixture in the team, driving the outpaced DBR4 Grand Prix Aston on four occasions, then sharing the Le Mans race-winning DBR1 with Roy Salvadori. It was the peak of his racing career, for he had already been diagnosed as having a heart 'murmur', and wound down his motor racing career only a year later.

By 1961, though paying the bills by running a Goodyear racing tyres distributorship, he was bored with a lack of involvement in the sport. According to legend, as a Consulting Editor to *Sports Car Graphic*, he spotted two press releases at the same time – one concerning the AC Ace sports car, the other about Ford-USA's new-generation 4.2-litre V8 engine.

Up until that time, Carroll Shelby and Ford-USA knew nothing about each other. However, having already been turned down by GM (for engine supplies of Chevrolet Corvette units), Shelby approached Ford, who were about to unveil their new 'Total Performance' marketing strategy. Ford guaranteed him supplies of engines for the conversion of AC Aces into what we now know as AC Cobras. Thus it was that Shelby's famous and profitable links with Ford were set up in 1961.

Less than two years later, with the AC Cobra project running smoothly, Shelby's development team repeated the shoe-horning trick, by building the very first example of what would become the Sunbeam Tiger. On this occasion, however, Shelby was never involved in manufacturing or distribution of the Tiger in the USA, and after a short time all further links with Rootes were severed.

Coincidentally, although Shelby lost touch with Rootes soon after Chrysler took a stake, the Shelby-Chrysler link was forged in the late 1970s, when Shelby's patron at Ford, Lee Iacocca, took over as Chrysler's chairman. At Chrysler, Shelby once again worked for his old patron, helping to produce high-performance versions of a major manufacturer's cars.

That, however, was after Chrysler had sold its European divisions to Peugeot, so there was never any further tie-up with the descendants of the old Rootes empire.

Back in Britain, racing driver Jack Brabham, who was not only a 'works' driver for the Cooper F1 team but also had a Surrey-based engineering business, was looking for ways to expand that activity. Having driven the four-cylinder Alpine for Rootes in North America, Jack realised that here was a competent chassis simply crying out for more power.

Having already seen Ford-powered Cobras on the race track, Jack suggested to Norman Garrad (his only contact at Rootes) that his business carried out a transplant job on the same basis. Unhappily for the genial Australian, he made little progress, even though there were several meetings to discuss the project.

Norman Garrad, though, certainly mentioned this to his son Ian, who was then Rootes's West Coast representative in North America. Quite coincidentally, Ian lived and worked in the Los Angeles area, close to where Shelby had his Shelby American business, and had also seen the way the Cobras had started to clean up in North American events.

Ian Garrad recalls thinking further around the subject, first by considering the fitment of various North American engines, including GM's aluminium V8 (which would later be taken up by Rover, where it was still being made in the late 1990s) – then dropping that idea when he discovered how physically large most of these engines actually were! At this stage, please note, no attempt was made to match engines to bodies, but a few measurements were certainly taken of these other engines in their normal habitat.

In the 1990s, some Tigers are more special than others! Work this one out for yourselves, for the 'Tiger' script on the flank is matched to pre-Tiger rear fins, and the special road wheels.

Harrington Alpines always look smart, particularly in a two-tone red and white colour scheme like this one.

Although the Harrington Alpine of 1961 might look as if it was inspired by the shape of the sensational Jaguar E-Type, the two cars appeared at the same time, which means that the Harrington's profile was settled before the E-Type appeared.

From this angle, every detail of the Kenneth Howes inspired Alpine style is pleasing. It seems a shame to add extra lamps and badges – but many owners did just that!

Earlier Alpines – this was an original-series car – had a neatly detailed and intergrated front end treatment, complete with headlamp hoods and bumper overriders.

Not all Alpines were red or white! This Alpine V is in a particularly attractive dark tone, and in more recent years the owner has added many options, including that rare fitting, a screen pillar mounted rear view mirror.

Extra fittings on this Alpine V are the pair of under-bumper reverse lamps, and the towing bar.

When the Alpine III gave way to the Alpine IV – this car being a IV – there was a simpler new grille style, and neat side lamp/turn indicators at the corners. As before, though, the top speed was still around 100mph (160km/h).

This nicely preserved Alpine IV shows off the revised style of optional hardtop which had been introduced in 1963, along with the very neat flip-up cap over the fuel filler neck.

When Rootes styled a new model in the 1960s, nothing was 'over the top', and nothing was omitted. What could be neater than this rear-end ensemble of a 1964 Alpine IV?

The boot of the Alpine III had a much better 'package' than original types, for the spare wheel was placed up against the bulkhead, and there were twin fuel tanks, one at each side of the stowage space (hidden behind trim panels in this study).

The Alpine's fins lasted from Series I to Series III (or 'Series 3', if you go by the badging!), for cars built up to the end of 1963. They looked extrovert, but were very practical, housing large and instantly visible stop/tail/turn indicator assemblies.

This Alpine III owner has fitted Minilite-style light alloy wheels instead of the pressed-steel types which were standard on all Alpines of the 1960s. Then (or now) these were very appropriate and popular in-period accessories.

Somehow we remember most Alpine Is as being white, but was this only because many of the official factory press shots featured a white car? This early example looks as good as it did in 1959, though the picture was taken in 1995. The wire-spoke wheels were extras.

This Harrington-bodied Alpine IV is a very rare beast, for it was produced in 1964, well after serious production of Harringtons had ended. Neat and nicely presented, this car has been somewhat 'customized' with Minilite-type wheels.

Although Rootes never sold these Minilite-style cast-alloy wheels as standard, they were used on the 'works' rally cars, and were definitely the 'in-thing' of the mid-1960s.

Tigers always looked the part, made all the right noises, and were even more purposeful when fitted with extra-wide accessory wheels. No sign of a V8 engine from this view, of course.

Look closely and you'll see the special '260' numbers in the Tiger badging shields, but from this angle there's no mistaking the twin-outlet exhaust system, which denotes the use of a V8 engine.

On advice from two friends, journalist William Carroll and racing driver Duane Spencer, he then emulated Shelby by turning to the new, lightweight, Ford V8. As far as Garrad was concerned, the new unit's major advantage was that it was relatively light (440lb (200kg) complete with all accessories), and because of its wedge-shaped combustion chambers it had compact cylinder heads, thus being several inches narrower than competing units. Even more significant, though no-one at Rootes could have realised this at first, was that the rear end of the engine (close to the bulkhead/firewall) was uncluttered, and that bulky, immovable, accessories like the distributor, oil filter and other components were all grouped around the front of the unit.

INVENTING THE 'THUNDERBOLT'

Garrad then made it his business to visit Shelby American and have a chat with Carroll Shelby himself. Having talked to Shelby and Ray Geddes (Ford's 'man on the ground' at Shelby American) on the basis of 'if we provided the money, Ford gave us permission to use its new engine, and you built a prototype, how long would it take and what would it cost?', an enthused Garrad then went away to raise support.

All this happened in February 1963. After first of all talking to John Panks, the director of Rootes Motors Inc. of North America (who would later go on to head up the entire Rootes sales team, and then become managing director of Automotive Products Ltd. in the UK), he then arranged for Panks to see Shelby and explore the possibilities, before getting more formal and suggesting the new project to the company's sales supremo Brian Rootes. At this

time Shelby had said a quick engine transplant development/design programme would cost $10,000.

Fortunately Brian had to attend a dealer meeting in San Francisco (which was little more than an hour's flight from Los Angeles), so Ian managed to corner him for what he later described as a rather serious evening drinking session in that city. There, during the boozy aftermath to quite a session, the two discussed the whole idea of a Ford-powered Alpine, before Brian Rootes eventually gave it his approval.

According to Carroll in *Tiger, an Exceptional Motorcar* (now long out of print), Brian Rootes then signed off by saying:

> Well all right, at that price, when can he start? But for God's sake, keep it quiet from Dad [Lord Rootes] until you hear from me. I'll work the $10,000 [£3,571] out some way, possibly from the advertising account.

The next day Brian Rootes and Garrad arranged to see Carroll Shelby along with Ford men Ray Geddes and Peyton Cramer, and within hours the deal had been done. Shelby said that he could have a prototype running in eight weeks. At this stage, please note, there was still no official factory backing behind the project – Brian Rootes having taken a flier on costs, without consulting his illustrious father and uncle!

In the end not one, but two 'look-see' cars were built, one to the original eight week schedule by Shelby American, the other as much more of a cut-and-shut job by racing driver/mechanic Ken Miles in his own garage at home. Miles would eventually join Shelby as an in-house 'works' driver, but at this time he had a small workshop of his own. Whereas the Shelby car cost most

The model and the Alpine III are joined on this occasion by John Panks of Rootes Motors Inc., of North America, who was one of the guiding lights behind the birth of the Tiger.

The Ford V8 engine was remarkably compact, though that high, wide and handsome generator fitting doesn't help. The distributor was, at least, at the front of the engine, which was a great boon to Rootes when trying to fit this unit into the Alpine's body shell.

of the promised $10,000, Miles is reputed to have delivered his part of the bargain for a mere $800, or £285, which was only about one quarter of the price of a complete Alpine car.

The 'Miles' car – originally a green Alpine demonstrator, but eventually painted bright red – was put together in no more than ten days, using a 260CID Ford engine which came equipped with automatic transmission – not the most desirable combination for a sports car.

Ian Garrad himself helped Miles during the second weekend, to get the job done. This particular car had the bulky Ford V8 engine mounted well forward, used electric cooling fans instead of an engine-driven fan, and retained the Alpine type of recirculating ball steering. No changes were made to the suspension, and no changes to improve rear axle location to cope with the engine's power.

As you might expect, this car had a very nose-heavy weight distribution figure, and did not handle as well as hoped. It suffered from axle tramp, but at least it showed the potential of the transplant.

The 'Shelby' car, or the 'white' car as it was later to be known, came together more slowly, and much more surely. Work did not even begin at the Venice workshops (not far from Los Angeles International Airport) until April 1963, which was just a year, as it transpired, before production would be announced.

Then, as later, Shelby American never pretended to be other than a small collection of bright, hard-working and adventurous 'can-do' engineers and mechanics. In the case of the Cobra which had preceded it, and especially in the case of the nascent Tiger project, there was never any question of making drawings, then building a car to those drawings. Instead the prototype would be built first, the installation prob-lems sorted out, and the formalities would follow.

Shelby, like Miles, soon found that the engine would just, and only just, fit into an Alpine engine bay. According to Carroll Shelby's own book *The Cobra Story*:

> I think that if the figure of speech about the shoehorn ever applied to anything, it surely applied to the tight squeak in getting that 260 Ford power plant into the Sunbeam engine compartment. There was a place for everything and a space for everything, but positively not an inch to spare...

Led by George Boskoff and Phil Remington, Shelby's team at least tried to get the engine as far back in the monocoque as they possibly could, and immediately blessed the fact that the high distributor was at the front of the vee.

Unlike Ken Miles, the Shelby team spent more time considering the weight distribution of the car, the way that the front suspension and steering had to be altered to accomodate the engine, and how to keep the back axle movement in check when it was being fed with the broad-shouldered torque of the Ford V8 engine.

This, of course, explains why Shelby's deal was worth $10,000 (though he apparently billed Rootes for rather less than this when the job was completed), and why Ken Miles had been able to do such a quick job on the other car. Ian Garrad and his boss John Panks were certainly impatient to see the car go on the road, but both eventually agreed that the wait was worth it.

Design Problems

When Shelby's team began to construct their car, several major problems had to be overcome, mostly due to the sheer bulk of the Ford engine. Although Rootes later claimed that the Ford V8 unit was only 3.5 inches (89mm) longer and two inches (51mm) deeper than that of its own four-cylinder Alpine engine, no mention was ever made of width comparisons. Although the new Ford unit was certainly narrower than any of its rivals (and, as Rootes would eventually find out, narrower than the British Daimler SP250, which was also briefly tried) it still filled the engine bay, almost to the exclusion of everything else.

Merely to make space for this engine, the water cooling radiator had to be pushed well forward – and it had to be a larger radiator than that of the Alpine.

This was the finalized installation of the 4.2-litre Ford V8 engine into the Alpine's structure. It was remarkably neat (the two might even have been designed together), and there was even enough space for the tubular struts from wheelarch to bulkhead to be retained.

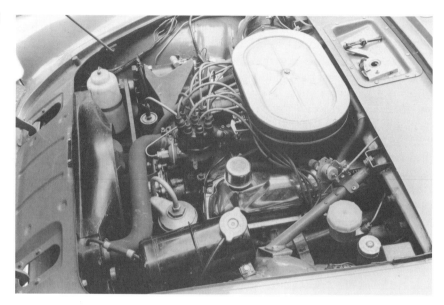

The solid Salisbury-type back axle for the Tiger, showing the original layout of the Panhard rod which helped to keep rear suspension movement in check.

This, though, was a minor problem compared with that of the steering gear. On Alpines (as on Minxes and Rapiers from the same family) there was a recirculating ball steering box hard up against the bulkhead/firewall (on the engine bay side of this panel), with a steering link across the back of the engine to an idler box on the other side of the bulkhead.

Steering box and idler box merely swopped sides between right-hand-drive and left-hand-drive cars. In both cases, track rods linked the steering/idler boxes to the steering arms on the front suspension units, which faced backwards.

This all worked very well with a straightforward, and quite slim, four-cylinder in-line engine between the two boxes, but when the 90-degree V8 engine was offered up, with its flywheel face back towards the line of the bulkhead, there was

absolutely no space for them.

Because Garrad and Panks insisted that the steering wheel and the column alignment had to stay in the standard Alpine position, this put the Shelby team into a real quandary, which took days to solve.

At first glance, a rack-and-pinion installation was the obvious solution, but as there was no such component in the current Rootes 'parts bin' the team had to look elsewhere. For this prototype only, an MG MGA rack was offered up – to the front of the suspension cross-member – but this was not an ideal solution.

Then, as on all Tiger production cars, the steering geometry was theoretically all wrong. In an ideal world, the inner joint of a rack's track rod has to pivot on a similar axis as the articulation of the front suspension, while in plan view the track rod should be squarely across the car.

For the Tiger, the familiar Rapier/Alpine type of front suspension/cross-member assembly had to be modified, to include the fitment of rack-and-pinion steering ahead of the cross-member pressing itself.

Because the Tiger's rack and pinion steering was so far forward (it could not be aligned any further back), there was a definite kink in the track rods linking the rack to the front hubs – and the geometry was by no means ideal as lock was wound on. Nowadays, of course, we would expect ventilation brake discs to be used – don't standards change?.

In this prototype installation, and in all later Tigers, the inner pivot was not quite ideally placed, and the whole rack was so far forward (front suspension assemblies on Alpines were mounted in a semi-trailing attitude) that the track rods had a considerable degree of trail angle themselves. Not only this, but it also meant fitting new type steering arms which faced forwards, instead of backwards as on the Alpine.

Although purists often looked at Tigers in later years and wondered how the steering could be acceptable (not only did the track rods trail, but they were bent too !), the fact is that the system operated remarkably well, which only goes to prove that what feels right is often perfectly viable. The fact that there was considerable tyre scrub on full lock (where the geometry deficiencies were most obvious) was usually ignored by Tiger owners – and it had to be ignored by the Rootes development engineers as there was nothing which

could be done about it.

Installing and keeping the axle movement in check was always going to be a problem. There was no way that the standard Rootes axle could deal with the massively increased torque of the Ford V8, so on the Shelby-built prototype a heavy-duty (and very heavy, make no mistake) Ford-USA Galaxie axle was fitted instead.

It was never intended that the Galaxie axle should be used on production cars, this merely being done to 'get the show on the road'.

Even so, there was still the on-going problem of the torque's tendency to wind up the rear leaf springs, and for severe axle tramp to set in. For the first few months after Shelby's car had been built, Rootes had to live with the problem, but before the end of 1963 a 'fix' had been developed, with the addition of a Panhard rod to locate the axle.

The rest of the 'cut, shut, weld, try again,

and build' job was relatively straightforward to achieve – no changes were made to the basic body shell, front or rear suspensions, or to the cockpit, for instance – and the 'white' car (as it became known) was ready for trial runs in and around Los Angeles on Saturday, 29 April 1963.

That was the day on which both John Panks and Ian Garrad sampled the car. As Ian later said:

> John and I left like a couple of happy kids and kept the car over the weekend, while we drove nearly a thousand miles, testing and evaluating the overall package.

Panks also got a chance to drive the other (Miles-built) car, then settled down to write a long report to Brian Rootes. This remarkable, closely-typed, six-page document made it very clear that Panks had fallen deeply in love with the concept of the V8 engined Alpine for:

> To say that I am enthusiastic is an understatement, for these are the most exciting and pleasant cars that I have ever had the privilege of driving... In short, we have a tremendously exciting sports car which handles extremely well and has a performance equivalent to an XX-K Jaguar... [By which, I am sure, he meant the E-Type Jaguar.] In summary then it is quite apparent that we have a most successful experiment which can now be developed into a production car which would enable us to gain a tremendous amount of publicity for the Sunbeam name... [And, at the very end of this submission, he added one sentence] I hope you like the name 'Thunderbolt'.

Brian Rootes, it seems, needed little further persuasion, but since no new products were ever approved at the Rootes Group at this time without Lord Rootes being content, it was necessary to persuade him.

It wasn't going to be easy. Lord Rootes, not even a regular driver by this time (he was usually chauffeur-driven everywhere in big Humbers), and certainly not a sports car enthusiast, was apparently very grumpy when he learned that this idea had progressed so far without him even being told, but he mellowed when told how much his son had liked the car.

Pointing out that he would agree to nothing until he and his team had tried the 'white' (Shelby-built) car, he agreed that it should be brought over to the UK for assessment – but promised nothing. Even at this stage, except for Peter Ware the Rootes design engineers were not briefed, and no time was allocated for them to study what Shelby had done!

Now the work really started. Over in America, lots more development driving followed before the car was packed away on a freighter ship for transport to Southampton in July. Ian and Lewis Garrad collected the car from the docks on a Saturday, drove it back to Coventry in an unlicensed state, and hastily prepared to show it off around the factory.

Competition Manager Norman Garrad was first to drive the car before it was sent up to Ryton for Peter Ware to try. He was too busy, whereupon it was ferried quickly back to Humber Road for Peter Wilson to see.

The legend, well-developed and re-told with embellishments, is that Wilson paced round the car, liked what he saw, drove off up the road and was so astonished by the performance that his beloved pipe fell out of his mouth and was ignored for the rest of the trip. Peter, who became a good friend of mine in later years, once told me that:

> That car's performance was quite unex-

pected, and I certainly didn't expect it to be as refined as it was. I'd driven a lot of racing and sports cars, don't forget, and I suppose I was expecting some crude lash-up that was all performance, but quite unsaleable.

The prototype Tiger wasn't like that. Shelby had done a great installation job, and it felt right, straight away.

With Wilson, second to Ware in the engineering heirachy, so obviously enthused, it was then easy enough to get Ware to break a few appointments and try the car. Once again, a world-weary engineer was astonished.

On this occasion, though, Lord Rootes not only insisted on seeing and sampling the car, but wanted to drive it himself, which was quite unheard of for a man who was already sixty-nine years old, and used to chauffeur-driven comfort.

When the noble Lord returned (having lost contact with his chauffeur, who had set off up the road in the Chairman's Humber to try to keep him in sight) he was also convinced. Before long he was intent on finding Henry Ford II to discuss engine supplies: legend has it that he tried to call Detroit at 10a.m. in the morning – which would have been the middle of the night in North America !

Fortunately for Rootes-Ford relations, HFII was on holiday, on a yacht in the Mediterranean, so once the two tycoons had got in touch a deal was speedily done. Over in Detroit his Ford Division Vice-President, Lee Iacocca, who was developing the secret new Mustang at that very time, was reluctant at first. However, once he realised that Rootes's forecasts of selling up to 8,000 cars a year were no more than his ambitions to sell the same number of Mustangs in a week, he backed down.

Then it was time to unleash Rootes's planners on to the car. How much would it cost? Could it be retailed in the USA for around $3,500? How long would it take to be developed? To be prepared for production? Where could it be manufactured?

Where To Build The Tiger? And How Quickly?

Most of their deliberations, in fact, were pre-empted by Lord Rootes. Not only did he agree that it should go into production, but he wanted it to 'go public' at the 1964 New York Motor Show, which was only eight months away.

Almost immediately there was pandemonium within the engineering and design departments, especially as work on the next version of the Alpine – the SIV – had only just been finished.

Roy Axe remembers that there was never any question of styling changes being allowed, and that the only thing which could be done was for new badges – the 'Tiger' script, and '260' shields – to be prepared. John Panks also wanted a new grille, an 'egg-crate' style, but this would have to wait until 1967 when the short-lived Tiger II went on sale.

By Rootes standards, to take a car from first running prototype (and even then, not even an in-house prototype) to public launch in *eight months* was unheard of, and many thought it impossible. No other British firm had attempted such an ambitious job and got away with it.

In the 1960s Rootes liked to take at least three years, if not four, to take a design from the 'good idea' stage to the showrooms, and close to final specification prototypes would usually be running two years before public launch.

[When the writer joined Rootes only six years later in 1969 (eventually to run the Product Proving operation), a year before the Avenger was launched there were more than a dozen prototypes already running around. What became the Chrysler 180 project was still at an early stage, yet nearly *three years* before deliveries began there were already seven prototypes in existence.]

In rather cramped surroundings at Humber Road, Alpine project engineer Alec Caine was directed to turn the Tiger project into a viable and cost-effective sports car, with Don Tarbun (who later worked for the author at Whitley) as his senior development engineer. It was always going to be a daunting task, but fortunately fate – in the shape of Jensen Motors and a half-empty factory – stepped in to ease the burden.

Almost from the day that Shelby-American finished building the original prototype Tiger, and John Panks had decided to urge its production, Carroll Shelby had hoped to get a contract to build production cars. That, though, was entirely premature, for although the project was already rushing ahead, no-one had thought that far ahead.

By late summer 1963, however, this was becoming one of the imperatives to be settled. The question was – should 'Thunderbolt' be built in North America, where the engines and gearboxes were to be sourced? Should it be built at Ryton-on-Dunsmore, in and among the conventional Alpines? Or should it be built by an outside contractor?

John Panks reported to Brian Rootes that there were three possible ways of having the car built in North America, one by Shelby American, one by Hollywood Sports Cars (which sold Rootes cars in California), and one by setting up a new Rootes operation.

The Shelby proposal did not really get very far. As John Panks had written in his seminal report to Brian Rootes, on 30 April:

Since driving the car in its completed form, Carroll Shelby has once again indicated that he would be most interested in providing facilities for production... He indicated that he would like to buy 100 Series III Alpine chassis in order to produce a trial run of 100 cars to enable us to make a dealer and public announcement, at the same time enabling production costs to be firmed up. His present facilities, which have been expanded to include a new building since your visit, are capable of this operation.

Unfortunately for Shelby, however, he had then gone on to press his case too far, suggesting that more radical modification of the Alpine's structure and chassis was really needed, and that his was the team which ought to tackle it. Panks also made the point that:

Shelby is terribly [closely] involved with the Ford Motor Company, not only with his Cobra and racing activities, but in addition he is doing a great deal of secret development work for Ford Engineering...

The other two North American assembly proposals were soon filed under 'castles in the air', for Hollywood Sports Cars, headed by Chick Vandagriff, had no manufacturing experience, but merely a yen to get involved in that sort of thing, while the idea of Rootes building up a new facility somewhere in the USA was rapidly abandoned.

Although it would certainly have been feasible to build the 'Thunderbolt' on the same assembly line at Ryton as the Alpine (and that possibility was seriously discussed), the third possibility, to have a British contractor build it elsewhere in the UK, soon took precedence.

Even so, in the 1960s, this was never going to be easy, as there were very few established concerns who could have tackled such a job. In the 1980s and 1990s, Lotus could have done it (they built Talbot Sunbeam-Lotuses, and Vauxhall Lotus-Carltons, of course), Tickford (which produced cars as diverse as the Ford Sierra RS500 Cosworth and the MG Maestro Turbo, both under limited-time contracts) could have emulated them, while TVR (who were so nearly hired to produce Ford's RS200s) might have been another.

In the 1960s, though, Rootes only knew of two sizeable businesses which could have taken it on – one being Thomas Harrington, the other being Jensen of West Bromwich. Looking back, it seems that Thomas Harrington, which had just finished building several hundred Harrington Alpines, was thought to be too small for the job – Rootes was already looking for 80 to 100 cars every week, which was well beyond the South Coast coachbuilder's capabilities – but Jensen might just be right.

There was a particular good reason for hiring Jensen, as Peter Wilson later made clear:

> As soon as it became apparent that Rootes were to build this new model, we had to decide who was to be responsible for undertaking the work. At that time Rootes had neither the space nor the experienced manpower to take on the project, so it was decided to sub-contract the work to Jensen at West Bromwich. Several factors influenced this decision, possibly the most important being the experience the Jensen engineers had with prototype development work and their capacity for being able to produce the car in sufficient numbers.
>
> Also Kevin Beattie, who was Jensen's chief engineer, and his assistant Mike Jones, had both worked for Rootes in the past so they knew our team and how we worked.

For Jensen and Rootes this was almost like a marriage built in heaven, for Jensen not only had the personal expertise, but they also had a sizeable and unused part of the factory, recently vacated by the Volvo P1800 assembly contract. Being in between development of new models of their own, they also had the capability to set up a production facility and manufacture, the 'Thunderbolt'.

Jensen, therefore, got the job, and Shelby had to be paid off. Jensen clearly did everything that could have been asked of them, for relations with Rootes (later Chrysler) remained cordial for many years. Kevin Beattie went on to become Jensen's managing director in the 1970s, while at the end of the Tiger project Mike Jones moved smoothly into Rootes, where he became the Senior Development Engineer on the new Avenger project, eventually working for the author for a couple of years in the early 1970s.

Ian Garrad then got the job of explaining to Carroll Shelby that the car was to be developed and manufactured in Britain, but seems to have accomplished this without rancour:

> Carroll already had his hands full with the Cobra and was comfortable with Coventry's decision. Over a handshake we agreed upon a royalty that he would be paid on every Tiger Rootes could build.

Shelby, the canny businessman, has never revealed what that royalty payment was, but since more than 7,000 such cars were produced, he must have been happy with the result. His effort, in fact, had been compressed into eight weeks in 1963 – but his rewards ran on into 1967.

Working at top speed with Jensen, therefore, Rootes raced to turn the Shelby 'Thunderbolt' into a production-standard

Jensen – Tiger builders

The Jensen brothers – Richard and Alan – founded their own body-making business, in West Bromwich (half way between Birmingham and Wolverhampton), in 1934, then sponsored the very first hand-built Jensen cars in 1935. Commercial vehicle coachwork was far more important than building cars at first, this situation persisting until the 1950s when the company gained its first important series production contract, to supply the Austin Company with two-door open bodies for the A40 Sports model.

Although Jensen's 'own-make' sales were still extremely limited in the 1950s (annual sales were no more than 100 or so), series production of complete body shells, later complete cars, built up rapidly. Factory facilities in West Bromwich expanded to make space for this, the move to Kelvin Way taking place in 1956.

From 1952, Jensen began building thousands of sports car body/chassis units for the Austin-Healey 100 (later 100-Six, then 3000) model, supplying these painted, glazed, wired and partly trimmed to BMC. Then from 1959, Jensen secured a contract to assemble the original Volvo P1800 Sports Coupé, starting with bare body shells supplied by Pressed Steel in Scotland.

When Rootes decided to start building the Tiger, management soon concluded that the car should be assembled by a sub-contractor. By this time not only did Jensen have a fine sports car reputation (Jensen work on the Austin-Healey 3000, and the Volvo P1800, was much respected), but there was also a personal connection, as Jensen's chief engineer, Kevin Beattie, had originally worked at Rootes.

Neatly and conveniently, Tiger assembly occupied the same facility recently vacated by the Volvo P1800, assembly of which had been transferred to Volvo's own factories in Sweden.

Tiger assembly was at its height when Jensen's Touring-styled Interceptor/FF models were introduced in 1966. After the Tiger contract came to an end, Jensen continued for nine more financially turbulent years, before being closed down by a Receiver in 1976.

---

motor car. All those involved remember the rush, but they also remember that Shelby had done a remarkable job in the first place, so this was clearly a straightforward (but not easy!) job.

The very first Jensen-built prototypes were still based on be-finned SIII monocoques, but as soon as SIV supplies became available at the end of 1963 the Tiger prototypes began to look like their eventual production counterparts. We now know that the Rootes/Jensen system eventually produced 14 Tiger I prototypes, of which one was the first Le Mans car (see Chapter 8) and one was sent to Carroll Shelby so that he could go racing in 1964, but only five of them were actually doing serious development work before April. In more ways than one, therefore, Rootes was living dangerously with this project.

Jensen's chief engineer, Eric Neale, looked after the building of the first British prototype, which was actually finished in mid-November 1963 (less than five months before public launch), the second car went to Cambridge for Brian Lister's attention, while the third was used to help prepare the Service/Owners' Manual information.

At first Jensen concentrated on the body shell changes which would be needed, and how best to mount the big (by British standards) V8 engine in the body shell. It was surprising just how many minor changes were needed to the 'hang-on' pieces of the V8 engine, which made it special as far as Ford-USA was concerned – water pump, crankshaft pulley and generation mounting brackets were all changed, the mechanical fuel pump was discarded, the oil filter relocated and (vital, this) one of the exhaust manifold castings had to be changed to provide a vertical outlet flange which did not get in the way of the steering column.

Somehow, more by good fortune than by sheer ingenuity, space was found to thread the steering column (left-hand-drive *or* right-hand-drive) down alongside the wide engine, and a newly developed rack-and-pinion steering (by Engineering Products) took the place of the BMC-type MGA rack of the Shelby prototype. Even so, the cranked track rod layout had to stay.

Most of the actual design work, though, centred around the rear end, where there were important rear suspension, spare wheel and battery changes.

Everyone agreed that the rear suspension and axle (which would be a sturdy Salisbury item as used in Jaguars and other British cars) had to be more accurately located. By the time the use of a Panhard rod was decided upon – which meant 'growing' mounts on the axle tube itself (simple enough) and on the inside of the monocoque's rear 'chassis leg' (not as easy) – this meant that the rod got in the way of the Alpine's vertical spare-wheel mounting position.

Accordingly, the wheel was once again laid flat (the original Alpine, don't forget, had used a very similar location, so there was no major problem in making the change), and at the same time the heavy battery was moved from underneath the 'occasional' rear seat to a place on the right side of the boot compartment.

In the engine bay Jensen used the redundant brackets vacated by the Alpine-type steering box and idler boxes (which were on the engine bay side of the 'chassis legs'), to hang the engine mounting brackets for the V8 engine, while a different type of rear mounting was used to support the gearbox close to the cruciform cross-brace. Surprisingly, the Girling braking system and 13in wheel installation was left alone at first, and although there was no doubt that bigger brakes and perhaps 14in wheels would have been desirable, neither time nor cost targets allowed this to be done.

Yet another variation of boot space allocations. On the Tiger the spare wheel was once again mounted in a horizontal state, under a movable panel, but much lower than on original Alpines, and for the first time the battery was located in the boot instead of under the floor behind the front seat. Suprisingly enough, this layout was never adopted for the Alpine.

Compared with the Alpine, there were virtually no changes to the Tiger's cockpit. Look carefully, however, and you can just see the chromed 'T-bar' part way up the gearstick, which was a feature included to allow the detent protecting reverse gear to be overcome.

A Date in New York – Just in Time!

By March 1964 most of the initial supply and technical problems had been solved, and the car had been given a name – Tiger. 'Thunderbolt' was dropped : some sources say that Lord Rootes suggested the name of 'Tiger', some that Panks took the honours, but all agree that the name was inspired by a previous Sunbeam Tiger, a racing car produced by the independent Sunbeam company in the 1920s. In this case, at least, a long and distinguished heritage had been valuable after all !

The engine and gearbox supply route from Detroit had been assured. Ford and Borg-Warner four-speed all-synchromesh gearboxes had been tried in testing, and although the first few Tigers had Borg-Warner boxes this was due to a supply hold-up, after which Ford boxes (the same

type, incidentally, as used in the Mustangs) became the norm.

There was just time to prepare one of the left-hand-drive prototypes (AF8 – AF, incidentally, being an acronym for Alpine-Ford) to showroom condition and fly it across the Atlantic, where it took pride of place on the Rootes stand at the New York Automobile Show in early April. This car was so new, and the project was still in such an early state, that it did not have the narrow chrome stripes which were fitted along the flanks of all Tiger production cars.

As with the Alpine SIV, the Tiger was to be available either in open roadster, or in closed GT form. Maybe it didn't have an ideal weight distribution (51.7 per cent was over the front wheels), and maybe it *was* quite a lot heavier – 2,653lb (1,203kg) instead of the 2,220lb (1,007kg) – but *Car & Driver*, when making an engineering

Tiger I (1964 – 1967)

Numbers Built
6,495

Layout
Unit-construction body/chassis structure, with steel panels. Two-door, front engine/rear drive, sold as two-seater open sports car, with optional steel hardtop.

Engine

Type	Ford-USA
Block material	Cast iron
Head material	Cast iron
Cylinders	8, in 90-degree vee
Cooling	Water
Bore and stroke	96.5 × 73mm
Capacity	4,261cc
Main bearings	5
Valves	2 per cylinder, operated by in-line overhead valves, pushrods and rockers, with camshaft mounted in block, driven by chain from crankshaft
Compression ratio	8.8:1
Carburettors	1 Ford twin-choke
Max. power	136bhp (net) @ 4,200rpm
Max. torque	226lb/ft @ 2,400rpm

Transmission
Four-speed manual gearbox, with synchromesh on all forward gears

Clutch	Single dry plate; hydraulically operated

Overall gearbox ratios

Top	2.88
3rd	3.71
2nd	4.86
1st	6.68
Reverse	6.68
Final drive	2.88:1

Suspension and Steering

Front	Independent, coil springs, wishbones, anti-roll bar, telescopic dampers
Rear	Live (beam) axle, by half-elliptic lef springs, Panhard rod, telescopic dampers
Steering	Rack and pinion
Tyres	5.90-13in cross-ply
Wheels	Steel disc, bolt-on
Rim width	4.5in

Brakes

Type	Disc brakes at front, drums at rear, hydraulically operated
Size	9.85in diameter front discs, 9 × 1.75in rear drums

Dimensions (in/mm)

Track	
Front	51.75/1314
Rear	48.5/1232
Wheelbase	86/2184
Overall length	156/3962
Overall width	60.5/1537
Overall height	51.5/1308
Unladen weight	2,200lb/1,007kg

survey a few months later, commented that:

> The Sunbeam has been utterly transformed by the change in engines, and it is a transplant that is all for the good... .All those concerned deserve a big pat on the back for having produced the Tiger...[including]...Lord Rootes for having the strength of character to do something that must run very much against the English grain, and all the people at Rootes for having put an automobile together so well.

But the Tiger had been launched, prematurely, in April. Production, in numbers – all for supply to North America – could not possibly begin until the end of June, which meant that customers would not see any cars until August at the earliest.

Would they be patient, and would the wait be worth it?

6 Tiger in Production

You have to look very carefully to distinguish a Tiger from an Alpine. This particular car has after-market road wheels to confuse the issue, but the standard recognition points are the thin chrome strip along the flanks, plus the '260' numbering inside the shield, and 'Tiger' instead of 'Alpine' script above the shields.

Once the Tiger had been launched, Jensen was impatient to put it into production, but that would not actually be possible until the end of June 1964. Having lost its contract to build Volvo P1800s in March 1963, a major section of its factory had gone silent, and workers had had to be laid off. Just as soon as supplies could be ensured, therefore, the assembly of Tigers could rapidly fill it up again.

It was one of the most ambitious con-

tracts which Jensen of West Bromwich had ever tackled, for there was more of the 'jig-saw' element in building the Tiger than ever before. Painted and trimmed bodies would come from Pressed Steel in Oxfordshire, engines and gearboxes would be shipped in from North America, while Salisbury of Birmingham (who were geographically close to the Jensen factory) would supply axle assemblies.

Hundreds of Rootes's normal suppliers

In one concentrated area of the front wing is all you need to see that this is a Tiger. The '260' numbering refers to the Ford V8 engine size in cubic inches – which we know more familiarly as 4.2-litres.

Very little space in and around the engine, in the bay of the Sunbeam Tiger. As you can see, the shallow air cleaner comes very close to touching the inside of the bonnet panel, especially when the engine rocks from side to side on its rubber mountings.

were then instructed to send components to West Bromwich rather than to Ryton, these including tyres from Dunlop, electrical items from Lucas and brakes from Girling, all of whom had factories in the Birmingham area, not more than an hour's truck delivery drive away from the Jensen plant.

Just as soon as the production 'pipeline' could be filled, Jensen began building up to 300 Tigers every month, a very similar rate to that of the Volvo P1800s, and carefully aligned to what John Panks's sales organi-

sation in the USA thought they could sell.

For the moment, as *Autocar*'s description pointed out in April 1964:

First production will go to America, and the car was announced at the New York Motor Show, but a right-hand-drive British version is to follow ...service facilities for the power section of the car are universally available, and a big range of performance improving kits is marketed.

Jensen set about building the Tiger in that

'can do' fashion for which they had so precisely been hired. As with the Alpine IVs, on which this car was so closely based, the body shells were pressed, welded, painted and trimmed at Pressed Steel in Oxfordshire before being sent up to West Bromwich on transporters.

At this point there was virtually no difference between the Alpine and Tiger models, except for the additional Panhard rod fixing stirrup on the right-side 'chassis rail' behind the line of the rear axle, the different boot layout with the Tiger's spare wheel lying flat, and the 12-volt battery living under a cover alongside it. However, no sooner had the shell arrived at West Bromwich when all that changed:

It was bad enough for experimental engineers to get the Ford V8 engine into that engine bay [Roy Axe remembers with a grin] but without change it would have been impossible for Jensen to produce the Tiger in numbers. I seem to remember that there was a stage at Jensen [it was one of the very first operations, in fact], on the assembly line, where a large gentleman with a sledgehammer had to step into the engine bay – high-tech engineering – to attack the bulkhead to make space for the Ford engine.

Swinging the biggest mallet I've seen, he'd pound an area of the Alpine-design cowl section back far enough to clear the Ford V8 engine. It was a lot easier than building expensive new tooling, and equally effective.

[This was the point on the car where the engineers later found that, no matter how hard they tried, the Chrysler V8 engine simply wouldn't go in.]

Even though this 'blunt-instrument' approach to the job – the panel involved, by the way, had already been rustproofed, primed, undercoated and painted by Pressed Steel, and no further rectification was done – was cheap and cheerful, it was

With the false 'boot floor' removed, this picture shows the spare wheel/battery location on all Tigers.

This restored Tiger, pictured in the 1990s, shows a facia well stocked with instruments, dials and switches. The radio installation was an optional extra, the fire extinguisher is a personalized safety item, and the steering wheel is an after-market accessory. Note the 'T-bar' on the gear lever.

actually the *only* way that Rootes could have considered changing the panel profile. To design, tool for, and prove out a new panel would have taken far too long, and would have cost a lot of money, in both cases this probably being enough to make the entire project a non-starter as far as the Rootes family was concerned.

Sales Get Under Way

Between 3 April 1964, when the Tiger was launched in New York, and the end of June, when the first production cars were slowly being assembled by Jensen, there was one vital commercial development that might, just might, have killed off the Tiger at birth.

Lord Rootes had done a deal with Chrysler. At a stroke, Detroit's third largest car maker, which had major European ambitions, had taken a big financial stake in Rootes, buying 30 per cent of the voting shares and 50 per cent of the non-voting shares.

Theoretically, of course, this meant that Rootes retained control, and that Chrysler had merely become a major investor, but in practice it meant that Chrysler would henceforth call all the shots, particularly in the North American and some overseas markets where they were already more powerful than Rootes had ever been.

The biggest embarrassment for Chrysler, which was obvious to everyone,

Britain contributed the racing chassis. America provided the mighty Ford V-8 power plant. The men in England who build the famed Sunbeam sports cars put chassis and engine together to create the hottest car to hit 1965. Test the Tiger's cat-quick reflexes. Touch the throttle and get the ride of your life.

This very carefully worded advert suggests that the Tiger might be the 'world's fastest sports car', but in fact in North America it was being claimed as the 'fastest sports car up to $3,499', which was an important difference. References to the Ford connection were later toned down at Chrysler's request.

Upbeat advertising from Rootes in North America for the Sunbeam Tiger!

was that Rootes had just announced a new model which was using a rival engine. Immediately before Chrysler took a stake in Rootes, the new Ford-engined Sunbeam Tiger had been launched.

It was, of course, too late to change the Tiger's design, though it would certainly have been possible to cancel the project altogether. That, however, would have caused considerable loss of face. Without a great deal of goodwill between Rootes, Ford and Chrysler, this could have escalated into an unbearable situation, so it was to everyone's credit that the car continued for the next three years.

At first it looked as there was to be an obvious way out – to substitute a Chrysler V8 engine for the Ford unit – but as soon as anyone tried to engineer a Chrysler-engined Tiger they discovered that it couldn't be done. In every direction, it seemed, the Chrysler engine was inches larger than the compact Ford: not even the smallest current Chrysler V8, a 182bhp (gross) /4,473cc Dodge/Plymouth unit would go in.

By the time cars had arrived in the USA, been shipped to the dealers, been readied for sale, and found customers, the North American summer was at its height. By the time the enthusiasts' magazines got their hands on a car, autumn was setting in, but *Road & Track* was so keen that it rushed through a full test, which was published in the November 1964 issue (which actually got on to the bookstalls early in October).

Rootes's 'bean-counters' had managed to do their stuff, and keep the retail price down below $3,500 (which Lord Rootes had thought so critical when he approved the project in 1963). Say what you like about Lord Rootes (and even those who were close to him, benefiting by his patronage, could often be scathing about his lack of taste), he was a marketing dynamo who knew his territories, and his public.

Little things like the decision to use 'Powered by Ford - 260' shields on the Tiger's flanks were meant to impress the Americans, and they did. Testers who knew

all about the Alpine – *Road & Track* published a report on the Alpine IV in the same issue – fawned over the Tiger's civilized specification, and soaked up all the 'made in the USA' fittings which made it special to them:

> In appearance, inside the passenger compartment, the only indication of there being something different about this Tiger is the stubby American-looking shift lever poking up out of the driveshaft hump. Otherwise everything looks very Alpiney...
>
> A tug on the hood release and lifting the lid over the engine compartment never failed to bring appreciative ooohs and ahhhs wherever we practiced this. Yes, you could say that there is little waste around the engine. In fact, you could say further that it fits very snugly. And, no, we wouldn't like to try to change the plugs – especially while the engine was hot.

Although *Road & Track* was friendly

Owners often fit larger than standard tyres, and special wheels, to their Tigers, to make them look even more sporty than when standard. As noted in the picture on page 113, the engine aircleaner is really extremely close to the line of the bonnet.

The Tiger on show at the Earls Court Motor Show in 1965. That 'Tiger girl' was only hired for the press day, which produced this remarkable shot. I presume that the Tiger in the foreground was stuffed!

enough to the Tiger, somehow they received it with an air of amused tolerance. Underneath the kind words, and behind the impressive performance figures, there was the distinct impression that they thought Rootes could do even better – and should attempt to do so very soon.

Nevertheless, Rootes (and Jensen!) built and delivered as many cars as they possibly could. According to one of several (different) sets of factory records I have seen, a total of 1,649 production cars were assembled during 1964, of which all but fifty-six were shipped to the USA and Canada.

Rootes had stated that all the initial pro-

duction was to go to North America, which indeed it had, but before the end of the year it is clear that a few cars were shipped to other destinations – and although British sales did not officially begin until March 1965, eighteen cars (presumably left-hand-drive?) were sold in Britain during 1964.

Before the unofficially named 'Tiger IA' took over in August 1965 – this really being the nomenclature for the 1966 model-year cars, when Series V 1,725cc-engined Alpine Vs began to be made too – a total of 3,756 Tigers were produced, with detail development changes being made throughout that time, including changes to the way the body monocoque was welded together (the same changes being applied to the Alpine, which was being made in larger numbers).

Rootes must have been delighted with the press reception generally accorded to the Tiger, especially as reports usually made at least one laboured reference to tigers, tails or roars! *Sports Car Graphic*, for instance, stated that : 'Very few will pull this Tiger's tail', which was typical.

It seemed, though, that Rootes couldn't please everyone all the time, for while some conclusions were that the Alpine had undergone a remarkable transformation, others suggested that it not gone far enough. Some (who presumably had no idea of what sold cars from showrooms) suggested that the Tiger might still be too civilized for its own good, while others wondered if the V8 engine transplant had made the Tiger too much of an animal.

By 1965 I was working for *Autocar*, based in the Coventry office, so I was lucky to get an early taster of the Tiger's habits. Taking delivery of the road test car in Coventry, before delivering it to London, was one of the many pleasures of a road tester's life at the time (as I recall, the 'return car' was something very ordinary like a Singer Vogue Estate Car, so it wasn't all glamour) – and it immediately gave me a chance to assess the Tiger's handling.

At the time, I vividly remembered the remark once made by BMC rally driver Peter Riley about the 'works' Austin-Healey 3000: 'If you give it a footful off the start line, it takes off in a straight line – towards mid-off!' Readers who understand the British game of cricket will instantly know what he meant; those who don't, need to have a translation, which was that the car veered off to one side as it gathered pace.

The location is the Motor Industry Research Association's banked track at MIRA, and the caption assures us that this pre-production Tiger was being driven by 'works' team rally driver Rosemary Smith. Note, by the way, that this car has not yet been fitted with its chrome strips along the side.

There's nothing like getting a celebrity to pose alongside your shiny new model – this being F1 World Champion Jack Brabham, and one of his single-seater race cars, alongside the first of the UK-market Tigers in 1965.

Even though the Tiger had a Panhard rod to hold down the rear suspension, it gave the same sort of impression, though the effect was often nullified by the Dunlop RS5 cross-ply tyres' inability to stop wheel-spin as well!

On less than dry roads, with any sign of gravel or mud, hard acceleration in a Tiger was an exciting business, but because the rack-and-pinion steering was so accurate one soon got used to dealing with it.

The UK-specification Tiger went on sale in March 1965, priced at £1,446, and there were the usually number of desirable extras including a hardtop for £60.42, and a radio for £29.18. By this time, at least, a heater was standard equipment, though one still had to pay £4.75 for a pair of static safety belts.

It was interesting to see that whoever wrote the *Autocar* description swallowed the party line about the 'works' rally cars being left-hand-drive because nothing else was available (it wasn't so – see Chapter 9 for an explanation – and it wasn't true either as the Le Mans cars had all used right-hand-drive – it doesn't always do to accept contemporary prose as gospel), and that *Autocar* mistakenly referred to the use of a Borg Warner gearbox, which had only applied to a few very early cars in 1964.

I remember contributing to the *Autocar* road test – as one of the resident staff in Coventry, I did more than my share of 'figuring' test cars at MIRA in those days – and liking it a lot more than the Austin-

The Tiger in the USA – stiff competition

When the Tiger was first marketed in the USA in mid-1964, it had to fight for sales against two other similar British sports cars. These were :

** Austin-Healey 3000: Recently updated to its final Mk III form, the 'Big Healey' was a long-established and well-loved sports car, with a 2.9-litre six-cylinder engine, and a 120mph (192km/h) top speed.

In mid-1964 its UK retail price was £1,106. It sold for $3,635 in the USA.

** Triumph TR4: Soon to be replaced by the independent rear suspension TR4A, the TR4 was the first of the 'Michelotti-style' TRs. Against the Tiger, it was rather breathless, because it only had a 2.2-litre engine, and a top speed of no more than 105mph (168km/h). On the other hand, there was a well-established dealer network in the USA.

At the time its UK retail price was £907. It sold for $2,849 in the USA.

** When the Tiger arrived in the USA, it was priced at $3499, compared with $2399 for the latest Alpine. When the Tiger finally went on sale in the UK in the spring of 1965, it was priced at £1,446.

Healey 3000 which I drove only a few weeks later.

Autocar's test car recorded a top speed of 117mph (187km/h) which confirms what I have already noted in the Alpine chapters, that the aerodynamic qualities of the Alpine/Tiger body style must have been poor, and it also confirmed that the engine transplant had not only transformed the performance but the weight too:

The penalty for this [engine transplant] is an increase in weight of some 4cwt [448lb/203kg], distributed evenly between front and rear. The effect is electrifying, with acceleration figures from rest to 80mph (128km/h) almost halved... Yet the Tiger is as sweet and docile as the best in family cars.

I think it was Geoffrey Howard who wrote the final words from the 'committee' opinions, and I can certainly agree with his comments on the traction:

We found the best technique for sprint takeoffs was to use about 4,000 rpm, to get the wheels spinning on dry tarmac, leaving only very short black lines behind. In the wet, rather more delicate control is needed to avoid violent axle tramp which, if allowed to persist, might damage the rear suspension.

Cornering on slippery surfaces calls for caution, as expected, although within a very short time one learns just how far the tail will kick out and to anticipate it early with steering correction.

In fact Geoff then went on for several more paragraphs to explain about the Tiger's habits. During the three weeks that the Tiger remained with us, several of us had all made thorough anti-social nuisances of ourselves when driving it. My own exhibition had been to bring the car back from Waterloo to the M1 one afternoon, via of King's Cross station, Camden and Golders Green, laying rubber at every set of traffic lights on the way. I remember doing this, but not why – except that I must have been in a singularly good mood that day.

It was therefore no wonder that we summarized:

> There is no doubt that the Tiger is somewhat misnamed, for it has nothing of the wild and dangerous man-eater about it and is really only as fierce as a pussy cat. A woman would find it easy to control. [That sentence would not be politically correct in the 1990s: sorry about that] Yet for the man who loves power it has a fascination, because it does all that it can do without fuss, noise or effort. It has a certain surprise quality too, most onlookers dismissing the car as just another Alpine until, suddenly, with only an impressive 'whoosh' it's gone, up the road and away before they have time for that second look. It's a car one parks with reluctance, such is the fun in driving it.

Later that year and in 1966, my editor, Maurice Smith, used the same Tiger (EDU 291C) as a day-to-day business car for 20,000 miles. For the second 10,000 miles of this stint, TechDel (better known today as Minilite) wheels were fitted. For Maurice, who had come to the Tiger from Jaguar E-Types and Aston Martins, this was a new experience, but he hogged the car, and would not often let us drive it, he clearly enjoyed it thoroughly.

All Tiger lovers should take time out to read this report for it will tell them more, with the experience and hindsight of a driver with vast experience of fast cars, than that of testers who may only have had a few days' driving of a Tiger:

> Some of the accounts of Tigers have been written after only a brief experience, and this is a car that improves with knowing... Some readers will also know Gregor Grant of *Autosport*, who has been agreeably surprised by his Tiger.

Those people who knew Maurice Smith well, and I certainly did for I worked for him for four years, know that he was quick to come to a judgement, rather impatient in his manner at times, but very loyal to those people or machines he liked: the Tiger was certainly one of those. He ended his report like this:

> Under-rated? The Tiger is judged by many, but known by few. Satisfactory and satisfying, it could prove itself to be the answer to many a keen driver's prayer. I am having another one.

And so he did !

Mid-Life Maturity

For Rootes, the 'few' – as Maurice Smith so thoughtfully pointed out – were probably too few, as the Tiger showed no signs of selling faster than cars like the Austin-Healey 3000 with which it had to compete. Perhaps it isn't quite fair to compare sales figures for a long-established car (the Big Healey) against a new model (the Tiger) but I will do so.

In its only two full production years, Tiger sales stacked up against Big Healey sales like this:

Calendar Year sales	Sunbeam Tiger	Austin-Healey 3000
1965	3,020 (North America 2,034)	3,947
1966	1,826 (North America 1,595)	5,494

The fact is that by 1966 the dead hand of Chrysler had begun to settle on Rootes Motors Inc. of North America, who certainly did not sell as many cars as they might have done if they had been able to put their full, and flamboyant, marketing effort behind the car.

Yet by late 1965, and the introduction of the 'Tiger IA' or 1966 model, the design was fully developed, the cars being that important bit more reliable, durable, and enjoyable than they had been when launched. Apart from the lack of interest in the car from Chrysler, though, Rootes's biggest problem was that the 260CID/4.2-litre Ford V8 was already obsolete, for all current Ford models using this engine were already using a more modern 289CID/4.7-litre derivative.

If the Tiger was to carry on in production, it would eventually have to use 289CID engines, and Jensen's predictions were that this point would be reached by the end of 1966. The 289 which was available to Rootes not only had a larger capacity, but was more powerful, with more torque. Here is a comparison :

260CID	4,261cc	136bhp/ 4200rpm	226lb.ft. torque/ 2400rpm
289CID	4,727cc	174bhp/ 4400rpm.	253lb.ft torque/ 2400rpm.

Incidentally, the 289CID engine produced figures which would have made companies like Jaguar very proud indeed, but in the case of Ford they represented the lowest state of tune available at this time.

With this in mind, all manner of other chassis and running gear up-grades were considered. Among the various major programmes evaluated by Alec Caine, Don Tarbun and their colleagues at Jensen at this time were:

    Automatic transmission
    Four-wheel disc brakes
    14 inch diameter road wheels
    De Dion rear suspension (using a
        Jaguar-style Salisbury differential)
    Relocated Panhard Rod rear suspension
    Radial ply tyres (at least as an additional
        cost option)

At the same time, John Panks began agitating from the USA for ways to be found of making the Tiger look different from the Alpine. Chrome strips, different badges, and twin exhaust pipes, after all, were not very obvious.

There then followed a long process of testing, of submissions to management and to the American dealers, all of which resulted in much posturing, horse-trading, and discussion of costs and pricing levels.

Accordingly, if you want to know why 14in wheels, rear disc brakes and De Dion suspension were never put on sale, you only have to know that all these would have pushed up selling prices to a level which Rootes's American dealers would only accept if there was to be a restyle too. And that, according to Chrysler, was out of the question on the current body.

For 1967, and what became known as the Mk II, the only style changes (and these were not very obvious) were the fitment of the egg-crate front grille which John Panks had wanted all along, the use of 'Sunbeam V8' shields instead of the 'Powered by Ford 260' shields of old, and the removal of the headlamp cowls (which must have made a marginal improvement to the aerodynamics, by the way).

According to the records, assembly of 260CID/4.2-litre Tigers ended on 9 December 1966 (when supplies of the engines ran out), after a total of 6,450 cars

Not all of these styling suggestions for the Tiger II were taken up. The speed stripe fashion was short and inglorious, the shield now includes a 'V8' message, and there is no chrome strip.

had been built. Yes, I know, for an industry which always worked in 'Sanctions' (which means that authority was invariably given for a large, round-figure, number of cars to be built before assembly commenced), that is rather an odd number, but there is no obvious explanation.

Incidentally, and just to confuse cynical historians like myself, that figure ties up exactly with the chassis numbers issued. I have written far too many books to accept this as more than convenience, for in many other cases certain numbers have not been issued. This time, however, Tiger enthusiasts should thank their lucky stars that it all ties up ! 1,649 production cars had been built in 1964, 3,020 in 1965, but only 1,781 in 1966.

TIGER II – A SHORT CAREER

Rootes's engineers were rather disappoint-

ed that the finalized Tiger II was little more than a re-engined Mk IA, with minor style changes, but the reason for this was immediately obvious when the USA price was fixed at $3,842 – significantly more than that for the Tiger IA. The dealers had been right – any further price increase would add complication and the price would have soared towards $4,500, which would have put it perilously close to the Jaguar E-Type of the day.

For comparison, in 1967 Ford Mustang prices started at $2,698 for the six-cylinder convertible version, and a V8 engine option added only around $200 to that. Allowing for the fact that most Mustang customers then loaded their cars with yet more expensive extras, this already made the Tiger II an expensive car.

The fact is that Rootes only ordered a small number of 289CID engines from Ford-USA, for the planners had already been warned that Chrysler might not allow

Rosemary Smith, with the famous blonde hair properly on show, posed against a studio backdrop of clouds, for the launch of the Tiger II of 1967. Tiger IIs were fitted with 4.7-litre/289CID engines, and had a new type of egg crate grille style. The headlamps hoods, too, had been removed.

Tiger 2 (1967 Only)

Numbers Built
633

Layout
Unit-construction body/chassis structure, with steel panels. Two-door, front engine/rear drive, sold as two-seater open sports car, with optional steel hardtop.

Engine

Type	Ford-USA
Block material	Cast iron
Head material	Cast iron
Cylinders	8, in 90-degree vee
Cooling	Water
Bore and stroke	101.6×73mm
Capacity	4,727cc
Main bearings	5
Valves	2 per cylinder, operated by in-line overhead valves, pushrods and rockers, with camshaft mounted in vee of cylinder block
Compression ratio	9.3:1
Carburettor	1 Ford twin-choke
Max. power	174bhp (net) @ 4,400rpm
Max. torque	253lb/ft @ 2,400rpm

Transmission
Four-speed manual gearbox, with synchromesh on all forward gears.
Clutch   Single dry plate; hydraulically operated

Overall gearbox ratios
Top	2.88
3rd	3.91
2nd	5.55
1st	8.00
Reverse	8.00
Final drive	2.88:1

Suspension and steering
Front	Independent, coil springs, wishbones, anti-roll bar, telescopic dampers
Rear	Live (beam) axle, by half-elliptic leaf springs, Panhard rod, telescopic dampers
Steering	Rack and pinion
Tyres	5.90-13in cross-ply
Wheels	Steel disc, bolt-on
Rim width	4.5in

Brakes
Type	Disc brakes at front, drums at rear, hydraulically operated
Size	9.85in diameter front discs, 9×1.75in rear drums

Dimensions (in/mm)
Track	
Front	51.75/1314
Rear	48.5/1232
Wheelbase	86/2184
Overall length	156/3962
Overall width	60.5/1537
Overall height	51.5/1308
Unladen weight	2,574lb/1,168kg

the car to remain in production for long. As we now know, Chrysler completed its takeover of Rootes in the first few weeks of 1967, and as I also now know, soon after this the order went out that assembly of Ford-engined Tigers must end when the current small stock of engines had been exhausted. In any case, Chrysler had decided that Tigers were not profitable to them, and that once the Alpine disappeared at the end of 1967 the Tiger would in any case have to be killed off.

The first production-line Tiger II was assembled on 23 December 1966 – immediately before Jensen closed down for Christmas – and series build got under way in the New Year, but by March it had fallen away to a mere trickle. The last Tiger of all was finished off on 27 June 1967, after a grand total of 633 cars had been produced.

[This was therefore not a good year for Jensen. No sooner had the Tiger line closed down, than Austin-Healey 3000 body struc-

To the end, Roy Axe's styling engineers were playing around with the detail of the Tiger's style. This car shows off the egg crate grille fitted to Tiger IIs, but the headlamp hoods are still present, the chrome strip has been removed (look very carefully and you can just pick out the line of fixings), while those look like the larger diameter, 14in, road wheels which were never fitted to production cars.

ture assembly began to tail off, and would also end in the autumn of 1967.]

Although Tiger IIs were theoretically never available to UK buyers, it seems that about twenty-seven such cars were actually delivered to British customers, though I am not sure how many of them were in right-hand-drive form.

We Brits, therefore, never knew if the much beefier Tiger II was a great car instead of just a good one. Months after assembly had ended, though, *Road & Track* of the USA published a short road test which showed a top speed of 122mph (195km/h) and 0-60mph (96km/h) acceleration in 7.5sec, and were clearly less impressed by the roadholding and hand-

ling balance than they had been three years earlier.

But it wasn't all bad news, for they summarized that: 'But if you treat it right, respecting it for what it is, the Tiger II can offer driving pleasure of a very high order.'

Maurice Smith of *Autocar*, having promised to buy a second Tiger, did so, and used a Tiger II for 16,000 miles. His car returned similar performance figures to the *Road & Track* car, except that it achieved 125mph (200km/h). Ending his report, which was published in mid-1969, two years after the assembly lines had closed down, he wrote that:

This Tiger could well become a classic of

its year and kind; most of us continue to like it, so maybe we will keep it running on and on and on.

It was a fine epitaph to a car which Rootes (which was about to become Chrysler United Kingdom Ltd) had already consigned to history.

Aftermath

Although Chrysler was not yet involved with Rootes when the Tiger was introduced, and was still only a minority shareholder for most of its life, it clearly rankled with the American concern that the Tiger was being powered by a Ford-USA engine. Well before the final takeover came at the beginning of 1967 it was clear that Chrysler would eventually become the overall boss of the operation, and that it already had a controlling influence over design and development policy.

To have used a transmission or an axle, maybe, would have been acceptable, but an engine, somehow, was so obvious, so public – the original USA-market brochures had made much of the Ford connection.

By this time Roy Axe had risen further through Rootes's styling and design hierarchy, and saw at first hand what was going on:

Chrysler either had to face up to the continued use of the Ford V8 engine, which was unacceptable to them, or they had to design an all-new car. For a time [this would be in 1966 – 1967] Chrysler put a reasonable amount of effort in its International studio.

This wasn't just a reworked Alpine/Tiger, but an entirely new car, a new-generation Alpine, which could be a Tiger as well. But the numbers – the financial numbers – just didn't work out. The more work they seemed to do, the less they could justify the product.

By then we were no longer working on the principle that Billy Rootes thought it was a good idea so we'd do it, and when nobody added up whether it was profitable or not until the end of the year. This was Chrysler bringing in those magnificent systems, which analysed the product (didn't they just!) and analysed everything to death, for that was their big problem at the time.

Despite a lot of work being done – not a lot of three-dimensional, but a lot of two-dimensional work – they ended up not doing anything at all. In fact the International department did quite a lot of work on the Tiger – they did some very exciting stuff which never saw the light of day.

Like other Rootes personalities I have talked to over many years, Roy agrees that the Alpine/Tiger model was killed off in 1968 because it had become an 'orphan' by then. Not only was it no longer a member of a family of cars which were still being made – in fact it was the last of the 'Audax' breed to be phased out – but by 1967/1968 it did not have many supporters in the company.

By that time, in fact, Peter Ware had retired, his place being taken by Cyril Weighell, who was an administrator rather than a motoring enthusiast, and there was also another personality, Harry Sheron, who had been given the job of Head of Design. Those people who worked for Sheron – and I was one, in later years – all agree that he was an efficient administrator and a very able businessman, but that he was simply not interested in sports and sporting motoring.

Once Chrysler had taken over completely, and the second Lord Rootes, Geoffrey Rootes, had become chairman, with Gilbert Hunt (ex-Massey Ferguson) as his managing director, Rootes rapidly became just a part of Chrysler, and could no longer operate as a proud family business.

Perhaps Roy Axe, whose team did so much, but suffered so many frustrations at this time, sums it up perfectly :

> If only they'd been clever enough to leave things alone, in the hands of people who could handle everything, if they'd taken more of a back seat and run the business better, maybe...

It would have been so easy for Rootes to cock up what they did with the Alpine and Tiger, and the miracle is that they did not. In the end I think the cars died because they didn't really know what to do with it, and they didn't really want to spend money on it, because whatever money they had, they wanted to spend on keeping their volume products up to date.

The Alpine and Tiger were always oddballs in the range. I think they didn't understand it, or have the same interest in it as in the family cars – I think it was as simple as that.

7 Alpine V – The Last Was Best

If you stood well back from Rootes in the 1960s, and understood how that over-stretched corporation worked, you could usually forecast which new models would be replaced next. The engineering department, in particular, and the planning departments, were too small to tackle more than one major job at once.

The arrival of the new Hillman Super Minx/Singer Vogue family of 1961 was a major undertaking, and the development of the rear-engined Hillman Imp (*and* a new factory in Scotland) occupied most people's minds in 1962 and 1963. Work on the new Tiger, on the massive facelift (or, should I say, the 'roof-lift'?) of the big Humbers, and in finalizing the new all-synchromesh gearbox for *all* medium-sized Rootes cars, meant that 1964 was also fully accounted for.

Alpine V (1965 – 1968)

Numbers Built
19,122

Layout
Unit-construction body/chassis structure, with steel panels. Two-door, front engine/rear drive, sold as two-seater open sports car, with optional steel hardtop.

Engine

Type	Rootes
Block material	Cast iron
Head material	Cast aluminium
Cylinders	4 in-line
Cooling	Water
Bore and stroke	81.5 × 82.55mm
Capacity	1,725cc
Main bearings	5
Valves	2 per cylinder, operated by in-line overhead valves, pushrods and rockers, with camshaft mounted in block, driven by chain from crankshaft.
Compression ratio	9.2:1
Carburettors	2 Zenith-Stromberg 150CID
Max. power	92.5bhp (net) @ 5,500rpm
Max. torque	103lb/ft @ 3,700rpm

Transmission

Four-speed manual gearbox, with synchromesh on all forward gears. Optional Laycock overdrive on top and third gears.

Clutch	Single dry plate; hydraulically operated

Overall gearbox ratios

Top	3.89
3rd	5.04
2nd	7.74
1st	12.14
Reverse	13.01
Final drive	3.89:1

Overdrive (Laycock) was optional, on top and third gears, when final drive ratio became 4.22:1. Overall transmission ratios were:

Top (O/D)	3.39
Top (direct)	4.22
3rd (O/D)	4.39
3rd (direct)	5.47
2nd	8.40
1st	13.17
Reverse	14.01
Final drive	4.22:1

Note : There was no automatic transmission option on this car.

Suspension and steering

Front	Independent, coil springs, wishbones, anti-roll bar, telescopic dampers
Rear	Live (beam) axle, by half-elliptic leaf springs, telescopic dampers
Steering	Recirculating ball
Tyres	5.90-13in cross-ply
Wheels	Steel disc, bolt-on, or optional centre-lock wire spoke
Rim width	4.5in

Brakes

Type	Disc brakes at front, drums at rear, hydraulically operated
Size	10.3in diameter front discs, 9×1.75in rear drums

Dimensions (in/mm)

Track	
Front	51/1295
Rear	48.5/1232
Wheelbase	86/2184
Overall length	156/3962
Overall width	60.5/1537
Overall height	51.5/1308m
Unladen weight	2,200lb/1,007kg

The next and, as it turned out, the last of the Alpines – the Alpine V – did not therefore arrive until the end of 1965. By any standards this was to be the nicest Alpine of all, faster, more torquey and even better built than any of its ancestors.

The biggest change made by Rootes in 1965, for the 1966 model year, was to introduce a larger version of the Minx/Rapier/Alpine engine, with capacity increased from 1,592cc to 1,725cc. This engine, complete with its five-bearing crankshaft, was central to the whole concept of yet another type of Alpine.

1,725cc – THE FINAL STRETCH

Time now to go back into Rootes's recent history. The original version of the current medium-size engine had been designed in 1950/1951, and had gone into production in 1954. At that time it was a 1,390cc engine producing 43bhp.

By 1961/1962, therefore, it had been in production for seven years, the size had increased by 14 per cent to 1,592 cc, but the peak power of the Alpine was up to 82bhp, which was close to a 100 per cent improvement on 1954.

Rootes's sales departments, however, wanted more, for this was the period in which every British manufacturer was producing more and more powerful engines. As far as the Alpine was concerned, too, a further performance boost was needed for the car to match its rivals in the all-important United States market. The new Triumph TR4 engine, after all, produced 100bhp, while that of the MG MGB (which would arrive in late 1962) produced 95bhp.

The problem was that the Rootes engine

You had to look very carefully to spot the differences between the last of the Alpines – the Alpine V – and early models. On this 1965 Alpine V, though, note the '1725' numbering inside the shield on the flanks, which is really the only clue.

You can't expect a 'classic' owner of an Alpine to leave it unadorned, surely? Not only does this Alpine V have the optional wire spoke wheels, but it also carries an extra rear-view mirror on the windscreen pillar, a badge bar, extra driving lamps and, naturally, the badge of the Sunbeam Alpine Owners Club.

already had something of a reputation. Reliable, sturdy and versatile, maybe, it was also well-known as a rather rough sounding and feeling design, and one which was something of an oil-leaker.

To remind ourselves, this is how the engine architecture had progressed over the years :

Year introduced	Bore × stroke (mm)	Cubic capacity
1954	76.2 × 76.2	1,390
1958	79.0 × 76.2	1,494
1961	81.5 × 76.2	1,592

Because of the cramped and parsimonious way in which it had been designed in the first place, there was very little space left in the cylinder block to enlarge the cylinder bore any further – not, that is, without re-coring the cast iron cylinder block to eliminate all the cooling water between cylin-

ders 1 and 2, and 3 and 4. That process, known as 'siamesing' was anathema to the designers, who feared overheating and block distortion.

Rootes may have been a bit backward-looking here, for BMC (with the A-Series and B-Series) and Standard-Triumph (with the latest Herald 1200 unit) were already producing thousands of engines every week with siamezed bores, and were reporting no problems. But there was great resistance at Rootes, which meant that the only way to enlarge the engine was by increasing the stroke.

After a great deal of soul-searching, therefore, the stroke was enlarged from 76.2mm to 82.55mm, the capacity therefore going up from 1,592cc to 1,725cc. This change, which sounds rather esoteric in metric measure, makes more sense when I point out that in good old Imperial measure the stroke had increased from 3.00 inches to 3.25inches – somehow, much more logical.

That extra quarter inch (measure it

Detail of the Alpine V's shield shows that the 'Rootes' title is still strongly featured. Chrysler would not be able to eliminate that until it took complete control in 1967.

between your fingers to get the point) looks tiny enough, but it was enough to produce all manner of potential problems at Humber Road, where the engines were to be built. As I commented in *Autocar* when describing the new engines:

> Because of limitations imposed by existing [machine] tooling, the cylinder block could not be deepened to accomodate the longer stroke, so the problem was solved simply by shortening the connecting rods by an equivalent amount.

When the first enlarged development engine was designed in 1962, the crankshaft still had three main bearings, and here the engineers had a rude shock. The increase in stroke, and the increased angularity of the shortened rods imposed greater out of balance forces, the result being a much rougher engine with vibration periods and character quite unacceptable for passenger cars.

The engine design team, by this time led by ex-Vanwall F1 designer Leo Kuzmicki, therefore had to take a 'brave pill', go back to their drawing boards, and emulate Ford by developing a five-bearing version of what had originally been a three-bearing design.

In engineering terms, this was done very elegantly indeed, for it is virtually impossible to 'pick' a five-bearing from a three-bearing cylinder block. The new intermediate bearings, naturally, were located between cylinders 1 and 2, and between 3 and 4, and at 0.75in wide were much narrower than the other three (original) 1.37in wide bearings.

To match all this hidden enterprise, the crankshaft itself was new and, for the very first time in a Rootes engine, a spheroidal graphite iron cast crankshaft was specified. All previous Rootes engines had used steel forgings. Rootes assessed both methods, and concluded that the new crankshaft was actually two pounds lighter than it would have been as a forging.

This larger engine, of course, was not

The late model Alpines, particular the Alpine Vs, were very well-equipped and civilized sports cars. The Mircocell-based seats had a reclining mechanism for the backrests, static seat belts were available, and the steering column was adjustable for length.

merely developed for the next Alpine, but for all the medium-sized Rootes machines in the Hillman, Singer, Humber and Sunbeam line-ups. Prototypes were already running, and were photographed, by 1963, but it would be another two years before there was time, space – and the marketing need – to bring it into production.

For very obvious production reasons, there was a clean cut-off between the building of three-bearing engines and five-bearing engines in the summer of 1965, for several major changes had to be made to the machine tool settings on the cylinder block, crankshaft and connecting rod lines.

ALPINE V – AN ALL-ROUND IMPROVEMENT

A wave of what became known as '1725' Hillmans, Singers, Humbers and Sunbeams were all introduced in September and October 1965, the Sunbeam

Rapier and Alpine versions being the first to surface in the middle of September.

Alpine enthusiasts not only saw that the engines had been enlarged, but that the aluminium cylinder heads had been modified, with the use of 0.03in larger inlet valves, and there had also been some attention to the shape of the ports (motorsport experience had helped that particular development).

But there was more. The higher-revving aluminium-headed engines were given a Holset vibration damper on the nose of the crankshaft (which helped soften a rather troublesome vibration at around 5,100rpm, there was an alternator instead of a DC dynamo to generate electricity, and a more ambitious camshaft grind (with no less than 52 degrees of 'overlap' around Top Dead Centre) was also specified.

If you looked carefully around the engine bay, you found an oil cooler mounted close to the water-cooling radiator, but the most obvious visual change, unique to the Alpine

From first to last, 1959 to 1968, there were no major changes to the layout of the Alpine's facia instrument panel display. This Alpine V shows a familiar layout, with the speedometer and rev-counter immediately ahead of the driver's eyes. After the knurled centre fixing had been loosened off, the steering column could be adjusted for length. The radio/loudspeaker installation was a Rootes accessory, which many owners fitted after taking delivery of their cars.

at this stage, was that the old-style down-draught Solex Compound (dual-choke) carburettor had been discarded, in favour of twin constant-vacuum Zenith-Stromberg carburettors whose breathing was more efficient.

The new carbs operated in the same way as the old SU, but there were many different details, notably the fact that the manufacturing company was not controlled by BMC, which SU was. The original carburettor from which this Z-S carburettor had been finalized had been designed at Standard-Triumph at the end of the 1950s, then handed over to Zenith to produce, on the understanding that it could only be

used on Triumph engines (notably the TR4 and 2000 units) for a period, before becoming generally available.

Once it was offered to them, Rootes pounced, for the new Z-S unit did everything that an SU could achieve, was independent of BMC, and was apparently a whole lot cheaper into the bargain, Z-S units would soon be found on many other Rootes models, sporting or purely family cars, but the Alpine V was the pioneer.

The result of the increased engine size, the new carburation and the different camshaft grind, meant that there was a significant power increase.

By the mid-1960s Rootes was having to crash test its cars, to make sure that they would meet the 30mph-into-barrier test (48km/h) which were being standardized in many countries. This is the result of throwing a sleek and desirable Alpine V into the unyielding barrier at MIRA in 1966. The engineers, however, seem to have done a good job, for there doesn't seem to be much distortion behind the front wheel lines, and the twin Zenith-Stromberg carburetted engine is still in one piece. The stiffening struts from wheelarch to bulkhead, too, have retained their integrity.

Model	Engine Size	Peak power (bhp)	Peak torque (lb/ft)
Alpine IV	1,592cc	82 @ 5,200rpm	94 @ 3,800rpm
Alpine V	1,725cc	92.5 @ 5,500rpm	103 @ 3,700rpm

Rootes was very precise about that half a horsepower when feeding information to the press, which was pedantic to say the least, as it was known that the production process was not at all accurate, that individual engines varied quite a lot, and that some of them were at least 5bhp below par!

Behind the engine there were no changes to the all-synchromesh gearbox, which had been a feature of the Alpine IV in its last year of production, though the short-lived automatic transmission (which had been introduced with such hope in the Series IV model) was dropped, as virtually no one had ever ordered it.

Those of us who were true sports car enthusiasts could see why this was so, especially as the Alpine had never had a surplus of power to deal with the power losses which were inevitable with Borg Warner automatic transmission, but Rootes's marketing staff were apparently nonplussed. Later in the 1960s BMC tried the same trick with the MG MGB, and that failed too. Until the mid-1970s, Triumph never offered automatic transmission with the TR sports cars.

Visually the Alpine V looked almost identical to the ousted Mk IV, except that the badging shields on the front wings (behind the wheelarch cut-outs) and the

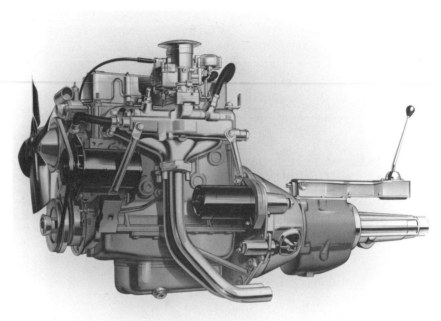

This engine/gearbox assembly shot has been retouched by Rootes artists. It shows us the familiar Rapier/Alpine engine in its last-but-one configuration, complete with a single downdraught Solex dual-choke carburettor. These engines are very strong, and for an accomplished mechanic they are very simple to strip and rebuild. Many spare parts are still available in the 1990s.

boot lid now read '1725' instead of 'SIV', this in fact being a new corporate symbol which appeared on various other Rootes cars fitted with the latest engines.

After all the performance figures had been taken, I used the *Autocar* road test car to rush round Europe in the wake of the 1966 Tulip rally (an event so nearly won by Peter Harper in his 'works' Tiger – see Chapter 9), and as a long-time fan of the Alpine V was surprised to find that this particular car really felt no faster than the last of the Series IVs.

Somewhere along the way, I concluded, either the Series IV engine had been stronger than advertised, or that this particular new Series V was not as good as the claimed figures suggested. Whatever the reason, this road test car still could not reach 100mph (160km/h) in both directions – a one-way maximum in three figures was spoiled by a figure of only 96mph (154km/h) into the wind (unlike the rest of the figures, this mark was double checked

on the M1, early one morning, by me, when the Boys in Blue were not watching).

No matter, along with photographer Ron Easton, we both enjoyed our time in Europe, for this final Alpine, like all the previous types we had driven, was a thoroughly comfortable, brisk, and handleable two-seater sports car. Noticeable, though hardly earth-shattering in its importance, was the useful space behind the driving seats – still quite useless for carrying other than very small children, of course, but ideal for Ron Easton to stow his cameras, for me to stow a brief case, and generally to keep the front seat area clear (for there were no stowage pockets in the doors).

Visiting Holland, Belgium, France and Switzerland in May was a good way to learn all about the car, in warm or chilly conditions. I clearly recall that we ran with the soft top back on many occasions, that we bickered amiably for much of the time about radio levels, but were very happy with the Alpine's performance as a 'chase car'.

Looking back to the road test, which I wrote (though the final version was always a 'team job' in those days, much discussed and much refined before being committed to print), I see that I commented that:

Performance and economy improved, with less fuss. Close-ratio gearbox with optional overdrive gives a good choice of ratios. Comfortable ride and fully-adjustable driving position. Safe, predictable, handling and powerful, but heavy brakes.

Although we all thought this car still good value for money, a British buyer still had to fork out £51.35 for an overdrive, and £18.12 for a heater – and in my experience no British driver ever did without heat, even if he did without overdrive !

Reading that test once again confirms that the last of the Alpines was like all the other front-engine/rear-drive Rootes-mobiles of its day – well-developed, carefully-specified, but without any extremes. None of us had any wild enthusiasms for it, nor any major dislikes – and I know (because I asked) that this was what Rootes engineers and planners had always intended.

In my final remarks I wrote that:

Complete weather protection, comfortable seats and adequate luggage room, with docile road manners and close to 100mph (160km/h) are now demanded by the enthusiast. The Alpine V provides all these and, although approaching its seventh birthday in July, continual improvements in equipment and power output have maintained its competitive position.

Even before they discovered that the Chrysler V8 engine would not fit into the shell, the International Styling designers had thought long and hard about updating the Alpine/Tiger for the late 1960s. This was a very meek and mild dress-up proposal.

Road & Track of the USA, Californian-based and still one of my favourite motoring magazines, got their hands on a non-overdrive USA-specification car during the winter of 1965/1966 (but then, winter in Los Angeles is usually very pleasant indeed), and published their findings in March 1966. Clearly suffering a little from a surfeit of Alpine tests over the years, the testers treated it as just another annual up-date (though they gave a lot of detail about the engine changes). Even so:

We got an honest 30mpg [USA gallons too – smaller than British ones] on an 800 mile trip at moderate cruising speeds and the worst tankful we used didn't go under 25mpg. This is excellent indeed and makes us wonder what might be possible in overdrive.

To sum it up, we can think of nothing more appropriate to say than that the Alpine V has retained the virtues of the previous versions and added a few new ones assure that it continues to be one of the most civilized of the contemporary sports cars. We like it.

So, too, did Jerry Titus of *Sports Car Graphic,* which headed its test with the sentence: 'When someone asks you: "Just what IS a sports car?", the Sunbeam Alpine is the perfect answer.'

The Final Years

Except that it was the important donor car for the Tiger (whose career has already been described), the Alpine V was fast becoming a forgotten car at Rootes,

During 1966, Chrysler-Detroit went so far as to build this clay mock-up of a rebodied Alpine/Tiger, though I can't help thinking that excesses like the roll-over pressings would have had to be abandoned. In any case, surely that body line is too low to accept the existing engines under the bonnet?

especially to the design and development departments.

At Ryton-on-Dunsmore, where it was still manufactured, it took shape around the painted and trimmed body shell (as supplied by Pressed Steel), seemingly with very little effort. Yet demand was well up on previous Alpines, more than 19,000 cars would be produced in a twenty-eight month career – and at best this meant that about 35 Alpine Vs were being produced every day, about 175 cars a week.

Although the development supremo, Peter Wilson, kept a benevolent eye on the Alpine, and Alec Caine continued to beaver away on minor improvements he would like to see added to the specification, the most noteworthy improvements were for reversing lamps to be standardised from September 1966, and for the self-adjusting

rear drum brake feature to be deleted from November 1967.

Chrysler's influence on all Rootes matters had increased considerably while the Alpine V was in production. By 1965 (when the Alpine V was launched) Chrysler, which had taken a big financial stake in the Rootes business in 1964, was taking more and more interest in its new investment.

As I have already made clear in the previous chapter, the American company's first moves had been to send 'task forces' across the Atlantic to see what was brewing, and before long all manner of helpful 'suggestions' were being made. All the studies being done to improve, and eventually replace, the Tiger, were obviously of significance to the Alpine, but once the Tiger was pensioned off the Alpine really had no long-term future.

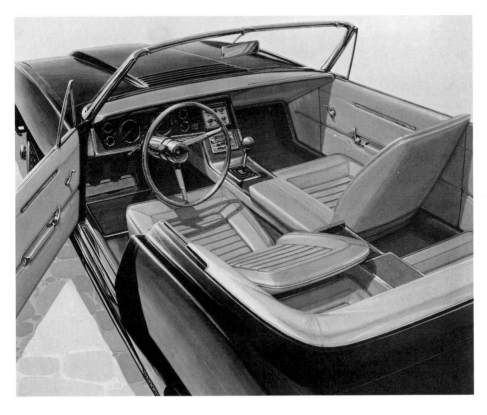

This was a 1966 Chrysler proposal for the facia layout of a rebodied Alpine/Tiger, which looks far more 'American' than 'European' to my tastes.

Once again for me, as a Coventry-based motoring writer, it was only necessary to see what new models Rootes (or should I say Rootes-Chrysler?) was developing at this time, to see that the Alpine was probably in trouble.

The short-wheelbase Husky, which had given its platform to the Alpine, was killed off in 1963 and not replaced. Then, in the autumn of 1966, a new Hillman Hunter/Singer Vogue family of saloons and estate cars appeared, these using the first of a new design of 'platform' from Rootes – the first major novelty since the birth of the Imp in 1963. Within months the old-style Minx/Gazelle models had been retired, while the last of the old 'Audax' family, the venerable Rapier V, also died in June 1967.

Incidentally, although nothing came of this, after the new-generation Hunter/Minx/Vogue/Gazelle cars had gone on sale there were tentative requests from the sales division that the old engine should be enlarged again, if possible. This was requested for two reasons – one because there was a totally new-generation engine already being developed for the Avenger range, and the other because several Rootes cars (notably the new-generation Rapier) were that irritating bit slower than some of their rivals.

I have certainly seen internal memos asking if the 1,725cc engine could be enlarged to 'about 1.9-litres' – but I am convinced that this was never attempted by the design engineers, who knew full well that there was really no further 'stretch' hidden away which could be accommodated on the existing production line tools.

That left the Alpine completely isolated, stuck with an engine which was smaller and less powerful than those standard in the MG MGB and Triumph TR4A. The Series V was also the last car to use even the short-wheelbase remnants of the

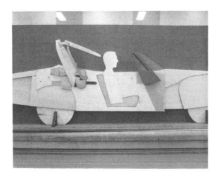
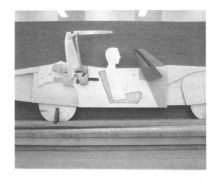
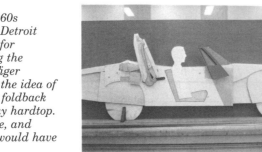
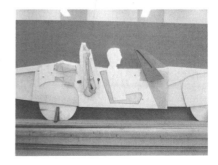

A mid-1960s Chrysler-Detroit proposal for rebodying the Alpine/Tiger included the idea of having a foldback stow-away hardtop. Expensive, and heavy, I would have thought.

'Audax' platform, so if any type of commercial logic was applied, it could not have much longer to live. Early in 1967, in any case, there was a social occasion at which the Alpine's future (or rather, its lack of future) was also spelt out to me.

Following the final Chrysler takeover, a group of us motoring writers met the new Rootes/Chrysler chief executive, Gilbert Hunt. In the middle of an affable conversation with him, I mentioned the Alpine, commented that its marketing seemed to be running down, but suggested that at least it must have made some money for Rootes in the past?

Hunt, a businessman rather than an enthusiast, looked at me, raised an eyebrow, pursed his lips, and made one short, and rather chilling comment: 'Not according to the figures I see, it hasn't.'

I knew then – and I did not have to wait for long for confirmation – that the Alpine's days were numbered. Pressed Steel, in fact, built the last batch of body shells before the end of 1967, but by the time they had been painted, trimmed, transported up the road to Ryton, and assembled, the last Alpine of all was not produced until January 1968.

So it was that the smart two-seater conceived by Kenneth Howes, and nurtured through so many crises by individuals like Peter Ware, Peter Wilson and Alec Caine, was killed off. In rather more than eight years, a total of 69,251 four-cylinder Alpines had been built.

Where are they all now?

8 Le Mans Expeditions – Successes and Disappointments

It was so unexpected, and so outrageously successful, that no fiction writer would have dared to offer it for sale. Would any publisher have accepted a story line which went like this:

Medium-size motor company with little racing experience enters the Le Mans 24 Hour race of 1961. Decides to use modified versions of its own production sports cars. Competes with two cars, gets one to the finish. Wins the Index of Thermal Efficiency award, which the French had invented to keep their own makers happy.

But it happened. For Rootes, though, the problem was that the Alpine's best performance came at the start of its racing career. From then on, it seems, things could only get worse – and they did.

Although Rootes had already built up a formidable and successful rally team by this time, as mentioned in the previous chapter, the 'works' team had very little experience of motor racing. Yet by this time the Rapier was already at its rallying peak, so following the Rapier's fine showing in British Saloon Car races in 1960, and at

Maybe it looks incongruous today, but in the early 1960s the 'works' Rapiers were extremely successful racing saloons in their 1.6-litre class. This was Peter Harper, at Silverstone, in May 1961. Much of the Alpine's racing specification evolved from these cars.

Norman Garrad – competition supremo

For most of the drivers who worked in the Rootes competitions team (the author was one of them), Norman Garrad was a somewhat forbidding figure. A tall man with an imposing manner, he was austere and businesslike rather than humorous, and treated motorsport as a demanding job rather than as a sport to be enjoyed.

A Scot who began his competition career in an Arrol-Johnston, he moved on to work for Talbot, and became a team driver in the famous 'Roesch' Talbot rally team of the early 1930s. When Rootes bought Talbot in 1935, Garrad went on to work on the Rootes sales side in Scotland.

After war service in the Third Armoured Division, he rejoined Rootes, becoming sales manager for Sunbeam-Talbot, almost immediately setting up the first 'works' rally team. It was under his control that the Sunbeam-Talbot 90 saloons, and the first generation Sunbeam Alpine sports cars, became so successful in International rallies. Only a determined Scot like Norman Garrad could have persuaded Grand Prix drivers such as Stirling Moss, Peter Collins, Mike Hawthorn and Graham Hill to drive on high-profile rallies without also paying them a king's ransom in compensation!

Later in the 1950s, the team turned to rallying and racing Rapiers, and then Alpines. With his son Lewis carrying out much of the administration – and, it has to be said, indulging in some very creative homologation – the team achieved much from rather ordinary motor cars. Not only did the Rapier become a formidable rally car, but the Alpine was most successful in events such as the Le Mans 24 Hours race.

By the early 1960s Garrad *père* was leaving most of the work to Garrad *fils,* and was clearly no longer at ease with the modern breed of rally drivers, and their professional habits. Although he might have been interested in seeing Tigers race at Le Mans, he was simply not interested in seeing slow Hillman Imps in rallies, so early in 1964, when still only sixty-three years old, he retired – which was when Marcus Chambers took over.

the International Compact Car Race at the USA F1 GP meeting at Riverside in November 1960, Competition Manager Norman Garrad and his son Lewis were encouraged to enter cars in more racing events.

As ever, this marketing push came direct from Lord Rootes, who could recognise glamour and excitement before almost anyone else in his Group. Nor was it done on a whim, for he, Brian and Timothy Rootes all wanted the company to get into motor racing on three fronts. In 1961, not only would Rapiers be used in the British Saloon Car Championship, but 'works' rally cars would tackle the gruelling ten-day Tour de France, and Alpines would be entered in the American Sebring 12-Hour race and at Le Mans.

PREPARATION – AND MODIFICATIONS

During the winter of 1960/1961, new 1.6-litre Alpines were speedily built up for circuit racing, but because the cars had to comply with Appendix J Group 3 regulations the initial modifications made were very speculative. Accordingly, the first test sessions – at a wind-swept Silverstone circuit in February 1961 – were not so much to prove the cars' pace as their handling and reliability.

According to the statement later released, the car had been very reliable, with most learned about handling, tyre wear and equipment in general. Rally drivers Peter Harper and Peter Procter did most of the work, while Mike Parkes (who by this time was more used to racing

Ferraris – even though he was still a Rootes employee, heavily involved in the development of the still-secret Imp family car) also took his turn.

Three new Alpine IIs then made the trip to Sebring in Florida for the famous 12-Hour race on the bumpy airfield circuit, and although there were high hopes, no one was expecting them to beat the well-proven MGA 1600s first time out.

The story of this race, in which there were sixty-five starters, is well-known. The two fastest Alpines, originally driven by Peter Procter and Paddy Hopkirk, jumped straight into the class lead (ahead of the 'works' MGAs), though the third car soon retired with engine problems.

As the hours ground on, however, the MGA of Parkinson/Flaherty and Peter Riley/Sir John Whitmore gradually overhauled the fastest of the Alpines, especially when it became clear that Dunlop's 13in tyres (as fitted to the Alpines) wore down much quicker than those of the 15in rubber fitted to the MGAs. Later this caused *Autosport*'s Editor, Gregor Grant, to note that: 'Sunbeams learned the hard way that time lost in the pits can lose races.'

The Hopkirk/Jopp car then blew its cylinder head gasket. Such was the length of the race, and the simplicity of the ohv engine, that Jim Ashworth's crew, led by the redoubtable Ernie 'Cold Start' Beck (the nickname came because of Ernie's unstoppable stammer, which embarrassed him not all, infinitely less than it embarrassed those talking to him) changed the gasket and sent Hopkirk back into the fray about one hour later.

The surviving car, driven by the two Peters – Harper and Procter – eventually suffered braking problems, but still managed to finish, third in their class, behind the two MGs. It was a good effort, which Rootes-USA managed to advertise by

pointing out that the Alpine had been fastest in its price class.

After that the cars were rushed back to Europe, and prepared to take part in the test weekend held in April on the Le Mans circuit.

Apart from their front and rear bumpers being removed and running with the production-type hardtop in place, both at Sebring in March and at the Le Mans test weekend in April, the Alpines had looked visually standard.

However, it was rapidly becoming clear that they were still not nearly fast enough – not only were they lacking in power, but their aerodynamic qualities were poor. As *Autocar*'s report on the test weekend commented:

> The Alpines, production-line cars driven by Peter Harper and Michael [Mike] Parkes, managed a best lap in 5min 16.5sec (92.93mph) (148.69km/h). This lap speed, when the car's maximum speed is little over 100mph (160km/h), is surprising, but there is scarcely enough margin over the 87mph (139km/h) or so which they will have to maintain in the 24-Hour race if they are to qualify as finishers.

At Le Mans, in fact, the Alpines had been much the slowest cars – twenty-four seconds a lap behind a 1.0-litre Abarth, thirty-two seconds a lap behind the twin-cam engined Triumph TRS (a prototype, admittedly), and no less than fifty-five seconds a lap behind the 'works' 1.7-litre Porsche RSK.

The Garrads, I know, were worried about this, especially because they realised that the aluminium-headed 1.6-litre engines had already reached their tuning limit. Unlike Triumph, who were running prototypes with twin-cam engines, Rootes were obliged to stick with the production unit

Peter Harper watching his Harrington-modified Le Mans car (3000RW) being prepared at Humber Road before the race. The mechanics are Jack Walton and Ernie 'Cold Start' Beck. YHP 288, in the background, was one of the team's current 'works' rally cars in 1961.

Pre-event scrutineering at Le Mans in 1961 – an occasion which caused Lewis Garrad a lot of grief because of the officials' obdurate attitude. It would have helped, he later said, if the cars had been French, not English.

and would have to find more speed else-where.

At this time I was about to join the 'works' rally team as Peter Procter's co-driver, and had begun to make visits to see Lewis Garrad at Ryton-on-Dunsmore, so I could see what was going on. I was also a recent ex-Jaguar employee, so in April, quite casually, Lewis pulled my leg about the effect the shape of the newly-launched Jaguar E-Type was having on his team's thinking. For Le Mans, he said, the Alpine needed to have a higher top speed. To do this, he said, they intended to adopt a more rounded nose with recessed headlamps, and a Harrington-style fastback tail – both of them, he pointed out, as near-copies of the E-Type coupé!

His engineers had also had a good look at the under-bonnet arrangements of the E-Type (no thought had been given to this on the Alpine production car), so every effort was going to go into managing the air flow into, through, and out of the radiator. Naturally he had heard all about Triumph's early traumas at Le Mans, when the TR3S cars had run with cooling fans, which eventually broke off, puncturing radiators, and causing retirement, so there were no such fans on the Alpines.

As Lewis later admitted:

> The cars weren't anywhere quick enough for a class win, which wasn't really so surprising at all. We came back from the test days and said [to ourselves] okay, we're not going to win, that's for sure. But if we do our job properly, we can make some petrol economy! We had another long talk with Engineering, and thought we could compete for the Index of Thermal efficiency.

Hedging their bets, Rootes had entered two cars for Le Mans, but in the event only one of them was modified along Harrington/E-Type lines. The line-up, accordingly, was :

No. 34   Peter Harper/Peter Procter
            'Harrington' shape car

No. 35   Paddy Hopkirk/Peter Jopp
            Standard shape car

As Lewis Garrad later told my colleague Richard Langworth, his team seemed to have more trouble in getting through pre-event scrutineering (which was always notably severe, nit-picking, and usually biased towards French crews) than through the race itself:

> We knew nothing about the intricacies of the organisers, who were the living end. For instance, we knew nothing about the rule that the boot had to have space for a 'standard' wooden suitcase fitted inside it.
>
> The Ferrari people were there [at scrutineering] at the same time, and they too were having trouble with the suitcase rule. In my very limited French I heard the Ferrari men say to the organisers: 'Look, that's sufficient as far as we're concerned, and you either accept it, or we go back to Modena.'
>
> They did! I thought – Blimey – if they can do it, so can I.

Lewis, therefore, also had a ritual, stand up row with the scrutineers, sided with Ferrari, got his way – and got through scrutineering.

After many last minute panics, modifications, and pre-event scares, the two cars were finally able to practise – they were actually five seconds a lap *slower* than in April – and were ready for the start. Incidentally, even though Rootes had looked at the E-Type for inspiration, they had effectively ruined the front-end aero-

Le Mans – the Fuel Efficiency category

When the French invented the Le Mans 24 Hours race in the 1920s, cynics said the event was specifically designed to show off the worth of French sports cars, but British Bentleys and Italian Alfa Romeos soon limited that aim.

Then, after the Second World War, there were no more large and fast French sports cars, so the organisers invented a further competition, a complicated Index of Performance event, which theoretically allowed small-engined cars (of which France had many) to compete against the big cars on a handicap basis. Even this was not always a guaranteed success for the French (Porsche was outstanding in this category), so the organisers tried again, this time with yet another category, to be known as the Index of Thermal Efficiency.

The classification was complex, for it not only included the average speed achieved by a car, but its scrutineered weight, and the actual fuel consumed during the race.

The Thermal Efficiency Cup was run for the first time in 1959, when a French DB-Panhard beat a Lotus Elite and the two race-winning Aston Martin DBR1s. The French were delighted. They were not best pleased in 1960, when the best of the DB-Panhards was soundly beaten by two Lotus Elites.

Then came 1961, when to everyone's astonishment the 'works' Sunbeam Alpine of Peter Harper and Peter Procter won the Category, beating a Lotus Elite and the fastest of the DB-Panhards. No wonder the French soon decided that this Category might as well be abandoned!

In 1961, incidentally, the Thermal Index was calculated according to a fiendishly complex formula. I can do no more than quote from a translation of the regulations:

The Thermal Efficiency Index is based on the relationship between the car's engine capacity, weight and quantity of fuel used during the 24 Hours. The calculations are as follows, the Thermal Efficiency Index being IR:

$$IR = \frac{Em}{Er}$$

where Er is the actual fuel consumption of the car in litres-per-100km, and Em is calculated from the following formula:

$$Em = \frac{P-300}{100} + \frac{V}{25} + \frac{(V-95)^2}{600} + \frac{(V-140)^3}{21,000}$$

V being the average hourly speed of the car for the 24 hours (in kph), and P being the weight of the car in kilogrammes (1kg = 2.2lb).

Apart from producing the most fuel-efficient engine and the most wind-cheating body style, it was almost impossible, and certainly impractical, for a team manager to prepare his entry with a view to winning this category. In any case, in the days before computers, it took far too long to work out all the combinations and possibilities!

No wonder Rootes were as surprised as anyone when they won the Index award in 1961!

dynamics by fitting two extra exposed driving lamps on the nose, along with sturdy brackets to accept the quick-lift jacks.

The story of the twenty-four hours of racing which followed, effectively is no news at all. The two cars merely went out, circulated, called for refuelling, went out, circulated, and so on, until the standard-shape car was disqualified at around half distance. This was because the Hopkirk/Jopp car was suffering from overdrive problems, then (according to Garrad, but not recorded in contemporary race reports) suffered an engine bearing failure.

According to the regulations some oil was added too early after a previous pit-stop. This was the sort of mistake neophytes make (only once though) but as ever the Le Mans organisers were not taking prisoners.

The two Peters continued to lap, never any faster than in April, which begs the question of whether the rushed Harrington modifications had been successful or not,

and spent only about nine minutes at their pits during the twenty-four hours. After two hours the gallant light green car was way down in 38th place, but had grabbed fourteen places before half distance, and finally finished in 16th spot overall.

With a fastest race lap of 5min 16.5sec, the Alpine had averaged 90.92mph (145.47km/h) over the 24 hours (it completed 2,182 miles(3,491km)) and except for the two very special 'works' Lotus Elites, was the fastest production-based car in the race.

That achievement alone would have been enough to set Rootes hearts singing, but to the team's delight the Alpine also won the prestigious Index of Thermal Efficiency award. Knowing that the Alpines had been remarkably economical in the Sebring race, the Garrads had always hoped to do well in this competition, but were still not certain that they could win it:

Lining up the two rather different looking Alpines at the Le Mans pits in June 1961. Although they shared the same running gear, No.34 had a much-modified body by Thomas Harrington, whereas No.35 used a standard shell with the optional hardtop in place.

The car was using very little petrol and causing no trouble. I remember at about nine in the morning, the chief organiser told me that if we souped our car up a little we'd beat Porsche for the fuel economy thing. Great delight! We ran up a sign that said 'plus 500rpm to beat X', and sure enough up came 500rpm.

Peter [Harper], of course, was very disciplined. The car just kept going round and round. Frankly we couldn't believe it! It gave us no trouble at all.

There followed hours of nail-biting tension (especially after the organisers' primitive computer broke down at noon on the Sunday) before the Sunbeam's victory was confirmed. Porsche, who thought they had won, finished well down, beaten by the Sunbeam, one of the Lotus Elites, and a DB-Panhard.

As *Autocar's* Harry Mundy later wrote:

Peter Harper's and Peter Procter's Thermal Efficiency Index win in the Sunbeam Alpine was praiseworthy and unexpected – particularly in view of its being the Alpine's first appearance at Le

This pit-stop shot at Le Mans is so relaxed that it must have been taken during the morning before the start of the race. Although the guest is unknown there are several well-known Rootes personalities in shot. Left to right: Lewis Garrad, Peter Harper, 'Tiny' Lewis (behind the pit counter), unknown guest, Paddy Hopkirk, and Norman Garrad.

An early action shot, Le Mans 1961, with the Harper/Procter Alpine ahead of a Ferrari 250GT Berlinetta as it races under the Dunlop bridge after the pits.

Mans. The car was the slower of the two: the Hopkirk/Jopp car had the advantage of a couple of extra hundred rpm, and was several places ahead of the Harper car when it was disqualified.

[Does this mean that the Harrington top and the faired headlamp nose was actually *less* aerodynamically efficient than the standard nose?]

For 1962 the factory prepared three Alpine IIs to compete in the Sebring 12-Hour race: all three were normal-shape hardtop models (with large fuel filler caps protruding through the rear windows – was this strictly FIA legal?), while there was also a privately-entered Harrington Alpine driven by two Americans. USA sales, and the right sort of image, were all-important to Rootes at this stage, so even though this was a boring motor race on a lousy, rough-surfaced, airfield perimeter track, the factory felt honour-bound to enter.

This time round, and armed with more experience that a year earlier, the team hoped to be a match for BMC's MGA 1600 Mk IIs, though they knew they could not outpace the 1.6-litre Porsches, maybe only outlast them. It didn't help that Peter Harper's car was pushed off the track in the early-corner mêlées, but fortunately this only resulted in body damage.

Although this was a battle of attrition, for which the Alpines were well-qualified, so were the Porsches. In the end the Alpines gave the MGA 1600 MkIIs a good beating – for the two Peters (Harper and Procter) were a full lap ahead of the Sears/Hedges MG team car – but they could not catch the Porsches, so had to be happy with third place in their class.

The good news, though, was that the leading Alpine averaged 74.97mph (119.95km/h) in 1962, significantly faster than in 1961, so real progress was being made.

Having built three brand-new cars for

Fuelling up the Index winning Alpine at Le Mans, using the vast filler neck poking out through the side window. By the relaxed body language which abounds, I am sure this was being done to the car before the race was due to start.

Winning the Index of Thermal Efficiency at Le Mans was sweet for the Rootes team, especially as this near-standard Harrington Alpine humbled the small-engined French cars in front of a huge French crowd.

Using a very standard-looking Alpine, complete with the optional hardtop but with front and rear bumpers removed, in the 1961 Le Mans race, Paddy Hopkirk and Peter Jopp lapped equally as quickly as the fast-back-styled Harrington car of Peter Harper and Peter Procter.

the Le Mans 24 Hours race in 1962, and following up this encouraging result in Florida, there were high hopes for the 1962 race. This time all three cars (9201RW, 9202RW and 9203RW) looked nearly standard, though their front and rear bumpers had been removed, and there was a sharply cut-off tail style which would never feature on any Alpine or Tiger production cars.

Because FIA Appendix J Group 3 regulations allowed it, these cars were even more special than the '91s, having perspex side and rear windows, and many aluminium (instead of steel) body skin panels. More work had been done on the 1.6-litre engines, and the Garrads hoped that the cars would be even more effective than in 1962.

One car (9201RW according to the registration number) turned up at the Test Weekend in April, where Peter Harper lapped it in 5min 8.6sec, and clocked 123mph (197km/h) in a straight line. Rootes stated that the body style innovations had reduced drag by eight per cent,

and the fact that eight seconds had been carved off the 1961 figures was encouraging.

Once again, in the race itself, the Harper-Procter car survived the full 24 Hours, while the second car (driven by Paddy Hopkirk and Peter Jopp) retired well after half-distance with a blown engine (the bearings had failed). However, although that car had lapped in 5min 5sec, which was a big advance on 1961, and the Harper-Procter ended up averaging 93.24mph (149.18km/h), this time there was no silverware to take home.

Compared with 1961, the Alpine had completed 56 miles (89km) more, and finished in fifteenth place, it wasn't placed in the Thermal Efficiency contest or in the Index of Performance category. Further, neither car was completely reliable, even in the first hours, for both suffered from sticking throttle linkages.

It isn't generally known that *both* of the Alpines suffered from engine big end failures. Damage to the Hopkirk/Jopp car's

For the 1962 Le Mans race the Harrington style which had been so successful in 1961 was abandoned, and a pair of more standard-looking Alpine hardtops were entered instead, with sharply cut-off tails. Note, however, the position of the fuel filler neck and cap, which protrudes through the rear window 'glass' – which would be perspex for the event. Car No. 33 was driven by Paddy Hopkirk and Peter Jopp (Paddy is driving at this moment); it retired with engine failure. The sister car (carrying No.32), was driven into fifteenth place by Peter Harper and Peter Procter.

engine was too serious for it to complete the twenty-four hours but, quite amazingly, the other car was brought into the pits, had its oil drained, then had its big end bearings changed in less than an hour!

Try telling your restorer that he, too, should be able to complete such a job, and make him tackle it in the same way, in the maelstrom of a pit lane, and that his mechanics should already have been on duty for at least sixteen hours before it was done!

Once the bearings had been changed, the engine was reassembled (rumours that the old engine oil, which had to be reused, was filtered through Judith Jackson's stockings were merely amusing tall stories – Judith was Peter's girlfriend, later to become his wife), the car was sent out again for a few laps to 'run in' the new shells, its oil was then topped up, and 9202RW carried on as usual.

Ponder, if you will, that the car lost at least eighty miles (128km), maybe ninety miles (144km), in this drama, then consid-

er that it later lost its overdrive, and the gearbox then started jumping out of intermediate gears – and ask yourself where it *might* have finished?

On the 'ifs, ands and buts' basis, a quick look at the finishing order suggests that the Alpine could have averaged nearly 98mph (157km), and that it could have taken 10th instead of 15th place.

Good excuses, of course, do not win motor races, and many years later Lewis Garrad was certainly not about to do the same:

We made a complete mess of it. We thought in 1962 that we knew it all – but money was running out, and we didn't have enough, really.

It taught me a lesson. If you are going to do something, do it well, because you can't go back to it after.

From here, unhappily, it was downhill all the way for with the Rootes empire gradually sliding into loss (the Hillman Imp pro-

The stripped out interior of one of the Le Mans Alpines shows the very large rev-counter fitted ahead of the driver's eyes. Full-race Microcell seats were fitted.

ject had a lot to answer for), promotional budgets came under increased pressure. Nevertheless, for 1963 the 'works' Alpines entered the same two races as they had in 1962, the Sebring 12 Hour race in Florida (two cars), and the Le Mans 24 Hours race (two cars – in fact two of the 1962 cars).

At Sebring there were local crews instead of British drivers, and although the cars set up a slightly lower average speed than in 1962, they still managed to finish third and fourth in their class. By Sunbeam Alpine, and Sebring standards, this was almost 'situation normal', so with no sign of the cars ever becoming dominant in their class they were not entered again.

For Le Mans, two of the three year-old cars (9201RW and 9202RW) were prepared. In fact one of those two cars had been quite busy since the 1962 race, for it had spent some time as a rally car, sometimes on the roughest roads and in icy, snowy, conditions (see the next Chapter).

It was not a happy occasion. One of the cars blew an engine in pre-event practice,

and both cars retired during the race with broken engines – one a head gasket failure, and one a broken crankshaft. For Norman and Lewis Garrad it was no consolation to know that the cars had once again been marginally faster than before if, that is, you can measure one second in a 5min 4sec (304 seconds) lap?

That, therefore, was the end of the 'works' Alpines' relatively short racing career. For 1964 there was a much more exciting prospect, the V8 engined Tiger, on the way.

TIGERS AT LE MANS – A SAD STORY

Looking back with that most useful of all abilities, hindsight, it is easy to say that the 'works' Tigers should never have been sent to Le Mans in 1964 at all. In such an undeveloped guise, they were never likely to finish strongly, they were never on the pace before and during the race, and they had both retired with blown engines after only nine hours of the 24 Hour event. Yet, was it all a disaster?

Normally, there would have been no sense in Rootes entering cars for the world's most high-profile motor race, without experience and before the production car had even been announced. But Rootes had been present at the three previous Le Mans races, with four-cylinder Alpines, so they could at least point to a good working knowledge of the Tiger's chassis, and to the idiosyncrasies of the event itself.

At this time, though, as I have already made clear, there's no doubt that when Norman Garrad initiated the programme, he was already under great pressure to deliver a result, as the Alpines were now at their peak, and the rally programme was 'between cars'.

At the end of 1963 the Rootes competitions programme was in transition. As rally cars, the Rapier saloons had finally been overwhelmed by more modern cars like the Ford Cortina GTs and the BMC Mini-Cooper Ss. In their third and last appearance at Le Mans, in 1963, the 'works' Alpines had been overwhelmed, and blew up under the strain. For 1964, in any case, marketing imperatives (and Rootes family politics) meant that the team would have to run Imps in rallies, even though they were totally undeveloped – too heavy and too slow by comparison with the 'works' Minis.

All this was very bad news for Competitions Manager Norman Garrad, for even a long-serving and successful company man like him could still fall foul of the imperious Rootes family if he was no longer seen to be delivering the goods, and there had been none of that since mid-1962.

It was clear that, whether he liked it or not, his star was on the wane. The fact was that Norman was already in his sixties,

was a manager of the old school, and one who had always demanded (and usually got) unquestioning support from his team – drivers and mechanics.

As a young co-driver in the 'works' rally team at that time I certainly sensed the 'gentry and serfs' attitude which applied, particularly to newcomers – especially when preparing to begin the 1962 Monte Carlo rally in Paris. Late in arriving to join my driver Peter Procter, to get a lift to the actual start, I appeared in the hotel lobby just in time to hear Norman snort : 'If he isn't here in one minute, we'll leave him behind. Let him find his own way. He'll have to learn!'

Not for nothing was he nicknamed The *Führer,* and not for nothing did he manage to get Grand Prix superstars like Stirling Moss and Graham Hill to drive for Rootes without paying them large fees. But he hadn't moved with the times – and, in particular, he hadn't managed to get Rootes to develop an 'homologation special' to match what their competitors were doing.

Someone who knew him well (and I don't think I should name him, for obvious reasons), told me recently that:

By 1963 I think it's true to say that he hadn't really kept abreast of the way motorsport was developing. Peter Wilson and one or two other people, at director level, felt that someone else should come in to run Competitions.

The drivers were certainly not in awe of him any more, in fact they were getting quite unruly. So, after all those years of success, he was unceremoniously moved sideways. He was moved back to the Sales Division, into some quite nebulous job.

He was not happy there. There was a lot of bad feeling about it. I felt that he was badly treated by the Rootes Group, and in his new position, for a time, he was quite a problem for his old department. I got the impression that he was undermining Marcus Chambers for some time.

He was very unhappy after that, and he soon retired.

Norman's son Lewis tells a rather different story:

Rootes wanted to take some of the weight off his shoulders, which is easy to do, shall we say, with a normal man. But Father, with such tremendous energy, didn't like it at all. He was broken-hearted initially, but he snapped out of it when he was put on special projects he enjoyed.

I moved off about six months before Dad. I guess I realised that a crisis was coming. The Rootes people were about to be married [to Chrysler] and in the event of a financial crisis the competitions department would be the first to go. I couldn't see any huge American corporation like Chrysler getting involved in European competitions...

Before Norman and his son, Lewis, moved out (which made it almost a clear-out of the old management team), they had lit the fuse on what was meant to be an ambitious motorsport programme for the Tiger – which, at that time, still had not received a model name!

Garrad's boss, running the Sales and Marketing Division for his uncle, was Timothy Rootes, who (as I have noted) was also destined to be much involved with the new Tiger's development and launch programme. Timothy and Garrad got together in the winter of 1963/1964, decided that the 'Alpine V8' had a good deal of promise, and worked out a proposed motorsport programme for the car.

Three special new cars were to be built, their first event was to be the Le Mans 24

Hour race – no pussy-footing about here, no minor event to use as a shakedown, but straight in to what was agreed to be the most gruelling endurance sports car race in the world. If the cars survived Le Mans with honour, they would then be prepared for the Tour de France (plans for this existed in the files when the new management took over), and a rally programme with more standard, off-the-production line, cars would then follow.

Le Mans and the Lister Connection

When I set out to write this book, Marcus Chambers agreed to give me a lengthy interview about his time at Rootes, then suggested that, instead, I used his own book – *Works Wonders* – published by Motor Racing Publications in 1995, to refresh my own, and his memory.

I want to acknowledge, here, that this has been an invaluable source – and I hope that it has helped to make the rest of this chapter completely authentic.

The new Competitions Manager was Marcus Chambers, who had already completed a glittering seven-year stint as Competitions Manager of BMC, but who had recently been taking a two-year sabbatical with Appleyard of Leeds.

Approached at the end of 1963 by Peter Wilson (who had been one of BMC's part-time racing drivers in the 1950s) to see if he was interested in the Rootes job, Marcus travelled to Coventry and was driven in one of the Tiger development cars before meeting Timothy Rootes and being offered the 'hot seat'!

I discovered that the company had entered two Sunbeam Tiger prototypes for Le Mans, [Marcus writes in *Works Wonders*] because they wanted to get as much pub-

Marcus Chambers: Competitions Manager, 1964 – 1968

Few British motoring personalities can have had such a varied career connected with motor cars as Marcus Chambers. Not only was he Rootes competitions manager from 1964 to 1968, when the Tiger Le Mans project was just getting under way, and the 'works' Hillman Hunter won the inaugural London–Sydney Marathon, but he drove an HRG at Le Mans, ran the BMC Competitions Department from 1954 to 1961, and had worked in colonial Africa immediately after the war.

Marcus – 'Chubby' as he was known by some of his closest admirers – was not only a great organiser and a technically proficient rally manager, but also someone who had a genuine interest for the sport. Like most such characters, he learned his craft by doing it, originally as a mechanic, then a driver, and finally as an administrator.

Because he was just as interested in having a good lunch as in getting to the next service point an hour early, today's motorsport fraternity would probably not understand him at all! He was a *bon viveur* in all respects, and no-one seemed to have a bad word for him.

Having spent seven years at BMC, where he had turned a shambolic 'Friends of Abingdon' club into the most professional 'works' rally team in Europe, Marcus then changed career direction and moved north to run the service department of one of Ian Appleyard's garage businesses in Yorkshire.

Tiring of that after only two years, he was contacted by Peter Wilson of Rootes (who was then second-in-command in the Engineering Department) to see if he would be interested in returning to motorsport. With Norman Garrad shortly due to retire, various factions were putting forward various names for this job – but it went to Marcus, who joined Rootes in February 1964.

This time he ran a 'works' motorsport team for nearly five years (his assistant for much of the time being Ian Hall), after which he was moved to the Engineering Department to administer the Proving Grounds operation, and to look out for a new facility for the company.

It was his last direct link with operational motorsport, for after leaving Rootes/Chrysler, he turned down the chance to run the Surtees F1 operation, worked for John Sprinzel for years in the retail motor trade, then retired to a beautiful Warwickshire cottage.

Even then he did not slow down. For the next two decades he took more and more interest in the historical side of the sport, writing many articles about racing and rallying, and finding time to revise and update his own autobiography, which appeared as *Works Wonders* (Motor Racing Publications, 1995).

licity for the production model as possible.

There were several contenders for the appointment, not least because there were a number of factions within the company, each with a particular axe to grind.'

Marcus then started his new assignment at Humber Road on 17 February, which was less than four months before the Le Mans race was to be run, and found that not a single car, not even a 'mule' had yet been built. 'The staff were demoralised, having had no leadership or well-defined programme for some time.'

One of them, one John Goff, is described

as a 'very abrasive young man, who later stressed that he was the competition department's resident engineer' – others have described him in less flattering terms – so he did not last long.

In the spring of 1964 the situation in the 'works' motorsport department was so bad that the new competitions manager, Marcus Chambers, must have been in despair. Having talked to Peter Procter (a team driver who just happened to be a builder, and lived close to Marcus's then home in West Yorkshire) he already had an idea of what was developing.

Ian Hall (Peter Harper's long-time

This was the first of three specially-bodied Sunbeam Tigers prepared by Brian Lister's racing concern so that Rootes could contest the 1964 Le Mans 24 Hours race. The shape looked near-standard from nose to screen, after which it had a special fastback profile.

co-driver), who joined the motorsport department as Marcus's assistant in April 1964, recalls that:

> We'd got nothing – we'd got the Imp, which was completely unproven, and we'd got a load of out-of-date family saloons. There had just been a Monte Carlo Rally in which I wasn't involved. It had obviously been a total and utter shambles, because they'd just run two or three standard Imps – those things would hardly pull themselves along. They'd also run standard Rapier SIVs, which were equally slow.

By this time, however, the Le Mans Tiger programme had already taken on a momentum of its own. Marcus found that Brian Lister's tiny business in Cambridge had been commissioned to build three special cars, and was amazed to find that although these were to have fastback styles, these were not based on the Harrington shape: 'A golden opportunity had been missed from the sales point of view', Marcus says, though I should remind him that the Harrington models had already dropped out of production.

Superficially, however, the decision to use 4.2-litre Ford V8 engines prepared by Shelby American of Los Angeles looked safer, for Shelby already had much experience of building highly-tuned versions for use in his own Cobra race cars.

In 1964 the problem was always one of time, for in February the first Lister-built shell was still not complete, the engines hadn't arrived from California, and the axles hadn't arrived from Salisbury's in Birmingham, so virtually no test running could be carried out before the Le Mans Test Weekend in mid-April.

7734KV (which was the test car, the only car at that point, and which would not race at Le Mans), actually went to Le Mans testing with virtually no mileage. Incidentally, haven't times changed – this car was not taken to France on a transporter, but actually driven there, on the public highway.

Le Mans Testing... First The Good News

Peter Procter and Shell competitions man-

ager Keith Ballisat were both at Le Mans to drive the car, and by drawing down a few favours, Ferrari 'works' driver Mike Parkes (who was an ex-Rootes employee) was also persuaded to sample the Tiger as well.

Apart from the Shelby engine's oil pressure being worryingly low, partly due to it running very hot, the car completed the weekend. The fastest time of 4min. 26.4sec (set by Mike Parkes) was around forty seconds faster than had ever been achieved by a Le Mans Alpine, while the recorded top speed was no less than 158mph (253km/h). This, at least, proved that there was nothing wrong with the Lister-inspired coupé shape, and that all the 275 American horsepower claimed for the race-prepared engines was probably genuine.

Although all the drivers complained about the roadholding, and clearly there

Keith Ballisat, not only an accomplished racing driver at the time, but on his way to becoming Shell's British motorsport manager, poses at Mallory Park with the test/development racing Tiger in the spring of 1964. Can you identify the script above and behind the front wheel? Is it a damaged (or purposely mutilated) 'Alpine' decal?

was work to be done on the cooling system (Des O'Dell eventually cracked the problem, but not until well after the Le Mans race itself), this was a mildly encouraging start. Marcus Chambers, however, had difficulty in convincing his management that since the Tigers were running as Prototypes, then they would have to compete against the Ford GT40s and the Ferrari 330Ps – one of which would almost certainly win the race, and which could reach more than 180mph (288km/h) on the Mulsanne straight!

Pre-event testing and development, sometimes at Silverstone, and sometimes at Snetterton in Norfolk (which was more convenient for Brian Lister's team), led to a car that handled better. During that process, incidentally, it became clear that Bernard Unett, who was still only a young development engineer at Rootes, was probably a faster race driver than any of those hired to do the job at Le Mans. Bernard, who later worked for me during my time at Rootes, was always happier behind the wheel of a racing car than actually working for his living (he will readily admit that, I am sure) and later bought one of the Le Mans cars and won many British races in it.

Although the two race cars – ADU 179B and ADU 180B – looked very smart with their long, Ferrari-like, fastback styles, these were still steel monocoques, and a lot heavier than everyone had hoped. This, as much as the lack of roadholding and development, was one of the biggest disappointments.

Most previous Alpine and Tiger histories have already pointed out that these cars were 66lb (30kg) heavier than a road-going Tiger. What is not generally realized is that the scrutineering weight of the lightest Tiger was 2,615lb (1,186kg), which compared badly with 2,088lb (947kg) for the

Ferrari that won the race, and even with 2,308lb (1,047kg) for the tank-like Ford GT40 prototypes. Only one other car in the race – the privately-prepared Iso Grifo – weighed more, and then by only 45lb (22kg).

To those of us living and working in Coventry, this was almost a rerun of the Triumph TRS Le Mans car saga, where in 1960 and 1961 Ken Richardson was obliged to run prototype twin-cam engined cars which weighed far too much, and which had shapes akin to those of a planned TR production car. The result, then, was a disappointment, and in 1964 it would be just the same for the Tiger.

Although they both looked extremely neat when they lined up at the pit counter for the race itself, we now know that neither car was completed until the week before the race, and had barely been shaken down, never mind run-in, before they had to be transported to France. The trouble started as soon as the cars began to practise, for one car immediately blew its engine, while the other was not as fast as the test car had been in April.

Marcus Chambers was all for withdrawing from the race, there and then, but was overruled by his 'elders'. Chastened, he therefore oversaw the engine change, installed 'chief engineer' Jim Ashworth in the passenger seat (Marcus had no time for Ashworth, thinking him to have been over-promoted years ago, and definitely a part of the 'old guard') and set off during the night to see how fast the car would go: 'We went down the road a couple of times and managed an indicated 150mph (240km/h), which at any rate proved that the headlights were adequate.'

According to *Autocar's* post-practice report:

The 4,181cc Shelby-tuned V8 engines produce 280bhp net, using the standard four-barrel Ford-Carter carburettors. Suspension modifications by Brian Lister include extra rear radius arms to take location loads off the springs. The cars were exceeding 140mph (224km/h) on the Mulsanne straight [If accurately timed by the organisers, this certainly proved that the test car had been faster in April] but the best lap time recorded was 4min. 26 sec by Peter Procter.

Team policy was to keep lap times down to a realistic race lap time, bearing in mind that the average lap time of last year's winner was about 4min. 18sec...

Unfortunately there was no happy ending to this story of hard work, but misguided endeavour. Neither car was really ready,

nor properly developed, for a race of this magnitude. Both the Tigers, driven by Keith Ballisat/Claude Dubois, and Peter Procter/Jimmy Blumer, made steady starts, achieving more than 160mph (256km/h) in a straight line, but were well down in mid-field, in the mid-twenties, as the event unfolded.

With the fastest Fords and Ferraris lapping more than thirty seconds a lap faster than the Tigers, they began to be lapped after about fifty minutes of the race, which must have been discouraging for the drivers.

In the meantime, the Shelby-built engines got no better as they loosened off, and low oil pressure (brought about, partly, by the sumps running extremely hot) was

In the early stages of the 1964 Le Mans race, Car No. 8 (driven by Keith Ballisat and Claude Dubois) rounds Tertre Rouge corner at the start of the long Mulsanne straight. Like its sister car, ADU 179B was forced out with engine failure, later blamed on poor preparation by Shelby American, who had supplied the units.

always a problem. After about three hours, the Ballisat/Dubois car suddenly expired, when a piston failed.

By half distance, the Procter/Blumer car had clawed its way up to a respectable 18th place and had been timed at 162.2mph (259.5km/h) (so the 'lack-of-pace' practice problems had been solved, after all), when its hard-pressed engine suddenly broke its crankshaft and the car suddenly stopped, opposite the pits.

Peter Procter was at the wheel, and remembers that:

> Just as I got level with the beginning of the pits the engine blew. I just remember a flash of fire coming out from under the bonnet. The steering locked absolutely solid – it was full of knuckle joints, and the engine had blown up in such a big way that it jammed all these, and I just couldn't move it a fraction of an inch.

I hit the brakes very hard and drifted over the demarkation line between the track and the pit lane. I gradually crept nearer to the pits, still going at quite a rate. Eventually I rubbed the car against the pit counter and stopped...

All this, incidentally, happened at 1.00a.m., in the darkness, but fortunately the pits were deserted at the time – to the great relief of Procter and the organisers. There was nothing for Rootes to do, but to pack up and return sadly home.

Marcus Chambers, being an experienced manager who had seen many triumphs and disasters in his motorsport career, bit his tongue when he returned to Coventry, trying not to say 'I told you so...', though everyone agreed that the failure was down to two associated factors – the failure of the engines, partly brought on by the temperature of the engine bays.

Car No. 9 (ADU 180B) was driven by Peter Procter and Jimmy Blumer at Le Mans in 1964. Blumer is at the wheel here. When the engine later exploded, with Peter Procter at the wheel just as the car passed the pits, parts flew out of the unit and jammed the steering, so that the car actually grazed the pit wall before it came to a halt!

More time for development would certainly have solved the overheating problem, but Ford-USA's engines had certainly let the side down. Reviewing the race afterwards, *Autocar*'s Ted Eves, who worked from Coventry and was close to the Rootes technical team in many ways, had this to say :

> On paper, the Ford return for the vast amount of money invested in trying to win the race was not good. Only two cars powered by Ford finished the race of the nine which started, but in only two cases were the power units to blame. These were the engines fitted to the Sunbeam Tigers...

Although the Tigers did not handle as well as the Alpines had done, this was hardly a factor at Le Mans (many cars, not least the D-Type Jaguars of the 1950s, have won the prestigious 24 Hour race with cars which did not hold the road very well), and everyone from Lord Rootes downwards was disgusted by the engine failures.

Since Rootes's highly publicized link-up with Chrysler had only taken place a few days earlier, this could not have come at a worse time, and it was immediately assumed that Chrysler would soon cancel a motor racing programme which involved a rival's power unit. That assumption was correct!

As we now know, the race car engines had not been tested, nor even debugged, before being shipped from California to Coventry, so in spite of Carroll Shelby's otherwise glittering reputation, this had been a very poor deal indeed. As Ian Hall recalls today:

> What failed were the Shelby engines, which were sent modern Grand Prix style in packages. The instruction was more or less, 'Here are the engines, stick them in

and race them.' We stuck them in – and they broke!

As Marcus comments:

> We were told by someone whom we could trust that he had heard that the Shelby test bed had been out of action for a fortnight at about the time when our engines were being prepared. Eventually we obtained a refund from Shelby, and no doubt it was used to buy engines for the rally Tiger.

After that the Tiger race programme was cancelled at very short notice, and although two of the three cars were sold off cheaply, one of them was retained for a time, and loaned to Bernard Unett to use in British events. Marcus remembers this car as 7734KV, while Bernard, who should know, remembers it as ADU 180B, which Peter Procter had leaned against the pit wall at Le Mans.

Bernard recalls that it was a 'pretty horrible car, with horrible handling. It was awful, very twitchy. The wheelbase was far too short...'

Even so, by spending a lot of time on development and preparation – by the end of 1965 the car had different suspension geometry, wheels, tyres, and a 360bhp 4.7-litre version of the engine – the Unett/Tiger combination was extremely successful, and won the *Autosport* sports car championship series.

If only the Shelby engines had been reliable at Le Mans in 1964, the cars might have achieved a respectable finish, but this might then have resulted in more racing outings and a much reduced rally programme. Although the Tiger's 'works' racing career was short, its rally record was much more impressive, and deserves a chapter to itself.

9 Alpine and Tiger – The 'Works' Rally Cars

When the time came for the 'works' to start building Alpines for motorsport, there was already a great deal of competition experience at Rootes. Even as early as 1956, Rootes had begun to use the Rapiers in rallies, and since the entire Alpine 'chassis' and running gear was Rapier-based, this was a real bonus.

Although by comparison with the dear old Sunbeam-Talbot 90, the Rapier looked to be a very ordinary car, Competitions Manager Norman Garrad was instructed to make it his front-line rally car as soon as possible. Introduced in October 1955, the Rapier had started its 'works' competition career in the Mille Miglia of 1956, where it won its capacity class, Jimmy Ray gave it a class win in the 1957 Tulip rally, then Peter Harper astonished everyone by winning the 1958 RAC rally outright.

Paddy Hopkirk joined the team for 1959, and finished third overall on the French Alpine rally, another Rapier won its class in the four-days-four-nights Liège–Rome–Liège, and with the arrival of the aluminium-headed Rapier SIII it became even faster and more competitive. A Rapier might not have had the pace of a 'works' Austin-Healey 3000 or a 'works' Triumph TR3A, but it usually had the legs of the factory-prepared Ford Zephyrs, and most other saloon cars on the European scene.

ALPINES IN RALLYING – FIRST EFFORTS

Once the Alpine had been launched, it was not long before Norman Garrad's competitions department started to build up a rally car. Straight away, though, I should dispel any idea that here was a big, glossy, well-financed and high-tech division: the truth was very different.

The Rootes competitions department, set up by Garrad on a wing-and-a-prayer in 1948, had always been based in an old brick building, tucked away into a corner of the ancient Humber-Hillman factory complex at Humber Road. Not only was there very little space for cars to be prepared – even into the early 1980s, when a descendant of this team won the World Manufacturers' Championship, a shop full of ten cars made it almost impossible to turn round – but the facilities were primitive, the floors were uneven, and for years there had really been very little input from the Engineering Department.

By 1959, when the Alpine was announced, the Rootes team had developed the Rapier (which was, effectively, the Alpine's 'sister' car) into a rock-solid rally car. In those days, as a young co-driver, often in Rapiers, I clearly recall the Rapier's habits – it was as fast as any other British rallying saloon, it handled remarkably well by 1959 standards (though the

Works rally drivers – heroes all

Let no one think that rally cars win events by themselves. They don't. Make no mistake, in any but a totally superior car (and the Tiger, unhappily, was never quite that), the driver had to work very hard for success, and his co-driver no less so.

The star driver of this Rootes period – as he had been for the previous decade – was undoubtedly Peter Harper, a Rootes dealer from Stevenage who had remained loyal to the Group when he could certainly have driven more competitive cars with rival manufacturers.

Starting in Sunbeam-Talbot 90s, but coming to maturity in Rapiers (he won the RAC rally in 1958), Harper had almost uncanny car control and great reliability. A remarkably smooth and fast driver, he always admitted that he never troubled to adapt himself to the sideways-Scandinavian way of driving a car on the loose – he was too much of a tarmac perfectionist, and a 'tarmac king'.

On the other hand, as his long-time co-driver Ian Hall recalls :

Peter could hold a car right on the edge – the ragged edge – without getting out of step, and that was truly amazing. His control of the throttle in winter weather was probably peerless. I genuinely believe that he could have had a better career in a racing car than in rallying.

I recall that on one of the few occasions he ever 'played away', he drove an unproven Ford Mustang in the ten day 1964 Tour de France – and won outright.

Rosemary Smith, she of the blue eyes, the mane of blonde hair, the endless legs, and the couture wardrobe, was usually underestimated, until she fought wheel-to-wheel in identical cars with the men, and was rarely outclassed. Her publicity image – the hotel lounge, the cocktail bar, the PR reception image – was carefully developed, but it was really all good camouflage for someone who had a steely will, great stamina, and considerable ability.

She rarely made mistakes, and usually brought the car home if it was still running. A string of good results in Imps, particularly in the 1965 Tulip which she won outright, tell their own story. BMC and Stuart Turner, I am certain, would have made more of the 'blonde in a sports car' possibilities.

If Peter Harper was the only true master of the Tiger, then Andrew Cowan could soon have become another. Today's master of the Mitsubishi World Championship rally team was still only a young Scottish farmer at the time, and if he had not annoyed Marcus Chambers more than once (by trying to get a crippled car to the finish rather than parking it) he might have got more of a chance.

Later, of course, Andrew proved himself by winning the 1968 London-Sydney Marathon in a much-modified Hillman Hunter, then innumerable rallies in the Far East for Mitsubishi.

Big, bald-headed, imperturbable Ian 'Tiny' Lewis is remembered by those of us who were there at the time as a patient and good humoured team companion. A Bristol-based motor trader, he could usually spare time to rush up to Coventry, or overseas, to take part in more testing, and he was a very useful development driver.

'Tiny' – so-called because he was so large – never won a major event, but came close on several occasions. It was 'Tiny' who retired his Triumph to let Geoff Mabbs win the 1961 Tulip rally, and it was 'Tiny's' Imp which finished close behind Rosemary Smith's identical team car when she won the 1965 Tulip rally.

What with Peter Procter (who so very nearly won the 1962 Monte with the author as his co-driver) drifting off to concentrate on racing, with veteran Peter Riley (who moved off to drive for Rover) and with a young Adrian Boyd coming up through the ranks, there was no shortage of talent available to the team.

front-wheel-drive Mini was about to move the goal posts), and it was by no means as fragile as some of its competitors.

As far as the Alpine was concerned, too, there was an added bonus, for a team of 'works' Husky estates – from which the Alpine's underframe had been developed – had already competed in one major event. The 1959 Safari!

Technically the Alpine's rallying prospects were therefore promising but, as in the retail market place, it would have to battle against larger-engined and more powerful sports cars, particularly the 2.2-litre Triumph TR3As and the 2.9-litre Austin-Healey 3000s.

Because Rootes was already committed to a full Rapier programme, it could not find the time (or the budget) to do more than dabble with Alpine preparation. Purely as an assessment of potential, therefore, a new car (Registered XWK 418) was prepared for the 1959 RAC rally, where it ran in hardtop form, with wire spoke wheels. Jimmy Ray, a regular team member (who had won the RAC Rally in 1955 in a Standard 10) drove the car, his co-driver being Phil Crabtree.

Rootes dealer Alan Fraser also entered his own personal Alpine, using a person-alised registration number (D63) which appeared on several Rapiers and Alpines in this period.

The story of the 1959 RAC (Blackpool to London's Crystal Palace, via Inverness) is well-known, for the result all revolved around a snow-blocked road between Tomintoul and Braemar. Those who tried to battle their way over this road (including Jimmy Ray) got stuck and had to miss con-trols, while those who went the long way round (including the author, co-driving 'Codger' Malkin's Rapier) and clocked in within a sixty minute lateness period, ben-efited.

Later runners also benefited by seeing cars streaming back from the blockage, but early runners, who had no warning, were jammed in for hours, including Ray, who had started at No. 15. Apart from not visit-ing those controls (only 15 crews reached the Braemar control within time limits), Ray and Crabtree were completely unpe-nalised on the arduous four-door route – and only nine crews achieved this. Theirs was a better performance in this wintry rally than *any* other sports car.

Protests and counter protests ebbed and flowed at the finish, but even though it had not been possible to use the intended route the stewards would not cancel the Braemar and Blairgowrie controls. The result was that Jimmy Ray's Alpine, which would have finished third overall if those con-trols had been cancelled, finished well down the list. As it was, Alan Fraser's privately-entered car (which had trekked 'round the moun-tain') was awarded 12th place.

Jimmy Ray, however, was an exceptional driver on slippery going, so this perhaps disguised the Alpine's sheer lack of power, which would be a handicap where road con-ditions were better. There was no way, it seemed, that an Alpine could be competi-tive on tarmac, so it was a real surprise to see John Melvin's privately-entered exam-ple winning the 1961 Scottish rally out-right. This, I remind you, was the era in which the Scottish featured driving tests rather than special stages.

Team Manager Norman Garrad seems to have reached these conclusions at a very early stage, for there were no other serious 'works' entries for the next three years. After its fine showing at Le Mans in 1961 (see the previous chapter), the standard-bodied car (3001 RW) was prepared as a road-going machine for rallying.

3001 RW started the 1962 Monte Carlo rally for *Autosport*'s Editor Gregor Grant

3001RW had already competed at Le Mans as a racing car before it was prepared for Autosport's *Editor Gregor Grant (in black hat) and Cliff Davis to use in the 1962 Monte Carlo Rally...*

...and, as proof, here is the car in the Competitions Department at Humber Road, alongside one of the team's Rapiers being readied for the same rally. Ernie Beck is working on the engine, which has just been installed, while Norman Garrad (in suit) and his engineer Jim Ashworth (in sports jacket) look on.

and his extrovert co-driver, London motor trader Cliff Davis, to drive, but although it started from Paris along with several 'works' Rapiers, the combination was never quick enough to figure in the results. Gregor, in fairness, was a better raconteur and all-round Good Chap than he was a driver – but at least he kept the rest of the team amused for a full week!

In 1962 the team repeated the trick. After competing at the Le Mans 24 Hour race in 1962 (where it finished 15th overall), 9202RW was reprepared, for Rootes's new Ladies' crew, Rosemary Smith and Rosemary Seers to drive. The glamorous

Ms Smith – tall, blonde, willowy, and always impeccably dressed – was originally written off by her rivals as merely a publicity gimmick (which means that the rivals wished they had thought of this one), which was quite wrong.

Ian Hall, Assistant Competitions Manager in the mid-1960s, recalls just how determined a driver she was and told me: 'Never, never, underestimate Rosemary. She was fast and she didn't crash.' (Later in the 1960s, of course, she also won the Tulip rally outright, after which the jibes disappeared for good).

The Alpine was outpaced on the 1962

Although this picture was taken nearly twenty years later, this shot emphasizes the limited space available in the Competitions Department at Humber Road.

RAC rally, where Rosemary finished well down (so why did another Sunbeam author claim she finished fourth overall?). It didn't help that at one point she slid off a muddy stage in Wales, and had to sacrifice an expensive suede jacket to help get the car back on the track.

Gregor Grant and veteran Fleet Street journalist Tommy Wisdom borrowed the same car for the 1963 Monte, but this was an event held in total 'white-out' – blizzard – conditions, and the dogged but no-longer-young crew ran out of time and energy.

There was just one final attempt with the Alpine, with Rosemary Smith in the 1963 Tour de France, an eight day event which combined thousands of hard road miles with speed hillclimbs and hour-long races at circuits all round the nation. Hers was a remarkably gritty performance, but once again there have been ludicrous claims in previous books about her result.

Rosemary and her new co-driver, Margaret Mackenzie, plugged on against all the odds (and against all the Ferraris!) in one of the bobtail styled ex-Le Mans cars of 1963, and not only won the Coupe des Dames award – which the gallant French thought extremely important – but eventually finished sixth overall in the Grand Touring category.

Starting from Strasbourg on 14 September, the event did not reach the finish in sunny Monaco until eight days

One of the 1962 Le Mans race cars, 9202RW, as ready to be driven in the 1963 Monte Carlo rally by Autosport's Gregor Grant (left) and Fleet Street veteran Tommy Wisdom. Rootes's works cars were nothing if not versatile.

Tommy Wisdom (at the wheel) and Gregor Grant had no luck in the 1963 Monte Carlo rally, where their ex-Le Mans Alpine II was swallowed up in the blizzard which engulfed most competitors.

later. One hundred and twenty-two cars started but only thirty-one finished (one of them being 'Tiny' Lewis's works Rapier), and in the GT Category Rosemary's Alpine was only beaten by three Ferraris and two very special Alfa Romeos, while she beat all eight Porsches and all three Simca-Abarths, not to mention a fleet of Alpine-Renaults.

By that time, however, Rootes had lost all interest in the four-cylinder Alpines, for there was a more exciting V8 engined version, the Tiger, on the way.

TIGER AND 200bhp: AN ENTHRALLING PROSPECT

It was no wonder that the 'works' competitions department were excited when they first heard about the new V8 engined Tiger.

Even in standard form its 4.2-litre engine would produce 136bhp, with peak torque of 226lb ft, and its potential had already been proved in competition cars as diverse as the AC Cobras and the Ford Falcon Futura Sprints. There was no doubt that more than 200bhp was available in Group 3 homologated tune.

Although morale in the Competitions Department was low at the beginning of 1964 (as I have already detailed in chapter 8), everyone perked up at the thought of rallying Tigers later in the year.

Assistant Competitions Manager Ian Hall arrived at Humber Road in April 1964, and immediately started trying to revive the rally team, and to get Tiger development started. Unlike the Le Mans Tigers, which would be racing as prototypes, the rallying Tigers would have to be homologated to compete as Group 3 cars in

Ford V8 power – so reliable, so light, so available

Ford's compact V8, which powered the Tiger, was conceived in 1958, announced in 1961, and in very much modified form was still being made in the mid-1990s.

In the late 1950s Ford-USA was using just two types of mass production engine – a straight-six and a V8, typically of 3.65-litres and 5.4-litres respectively. The 'six' dated back to 1951 while the vast and heavy Y-Block V8 dated from 1954. There was an even bigger V8, a 7.0-litre monster, used by the Lincoln-badged 'Big Fords' of the period.

Facing up to Chevrolet – as always – and because the 5.4-litre was scheduled to get bigger in the future, Ford decided that it needed a new 'intermediate' V8 engine for the 1960s and beyond, which would have to be a lot smaller and lighter than the existing 'Y-Block' type.

Rejecting the idea of using aluminium castings, but pushing its own foundry's 'thin-wall' casting knowledge to the limits, the new engine eventually appeared in the autumn of 1961, as a 221 CID (Cubic Inch Displacement)/3,621cc unit, or a 260CID/4,261cc unit producing a modest 145bhp or 160bhp, but there was a lot of built-in 'capacity-stretch' for the future. Initially used in the Ford Fairlane and related Mercury Meteor models, it soon found a home in cars as diverse as the Falcon and Mustang models.

Not only was this a very light engine by American V8 standards, it was also very compact (Rootes eventually found that no other V8 could be fitted into the Alpine/Tiger engine bay which had so comfortably received the Ford unit) – and very tuneable.

This was the engine which soon grew to 4.7-litres/289CID, was used by Ford as the basis of its Ford GT/GT40 racing units, for use in the 'works' AC Cobras, and for Lotus to use in its Indianapolis 500 1963 race single-seaters. It found its way into innumerable sports and racing cars in the next few years, into cars as special as the early 1970s Iso Grifo and DeTomaso Pantera Italian 'Supercars', and a formidable tuning industry grew up around it.

By the 1970s it had been enlarged to 5-litres (302CID), then in 'Cleveland' form with a longer stroke to become a 5.7-litre/351CID unit. Years after all the larger Ford V8 engines had been killed off because of the problem of meeting burgeoning exhaust emission regulations, the 'Cleveland' design soldiered on. As recently as 1995, final versions of this engine were still being used in the latest (new generation) AC Ace, Ford Mustang, Ford Bronco 4 × 4 and Ford Fairmont (Australia) types.

rallies. As I was a rival team manager at the time (at Standard-Triumph, on the other side of Coventry), I clearly recall that newly homologated cars could often be made to go much faster if the correct options were homologated.

But there were more basic problems to be settled by Ian Hall:

Marcus Chambers had just arrived, Norman Garrad and Lewis had both gone. Shortly, too, Des O'Dell arrived as a senior mechanic, straight from Ford Advanced Vehicles and John Wyer. Marcus brought him in, knowing that although Des knew nothing about rallying, he knew a lot about engineering.

In the next few years I like to think I taught him about rallying, and he taught the Rootes Group how to make its cars stay in one piece. Des was a practical, experienced, hands-on engineer/mechanic. He knew nothing about rallying at first – but he sat down to learn all about it.

By the time I arrived, the Le Mans cars were already built, and since it was nothing to do with me – I'd been hired to co-ordinate the rally team – I decided to have *nothing* to do with them.

At that stage it had already been

decided to run with the new Tiger in the Tour de France [Rootes was the first British 'works' team to take the very demanding Tour de France seriously], so I settled down to prepare recces and hotel bookings, which in the end we didn't need. That was mainly because Dunlop – we were contracted to them – got into a sweat when they found out that the Tigers would be capable of well over 130mph (208km/h) on 13 inch wheels! [On homologated cars, wheel diameters could not be enlarged]

Never mind. Marcus had already decided that a '4.2-litre engined Hillman Husky' – that's what some people called the Tiger – was bound to win some events purely because it had such a lot of poke.

In 1964 the Grand Touring/Sports car battle in rallying was at its peak. The 'works' Austin-Healey 3000s had 210bhp backed by eight years development, the Porsche 911s were just beginning to appear, while the ultra-lightweight Alfa Romeo GTZ coupés were also extremely effective on tarmac stages, so the Tiger would need all that fabled 'poke' if it was to succeed.

Although the race and rally Alpines had provided much information, the Tigers, by definition, were very different. Compared with the Alpines, they were twice as powerful, but only about 20 per cent heavier. There was never any doubt about their straight line performance, but would team drivers like Peter Harper be able to keep the chassis in check? An all-purpose recce trip to the French mountains in July, coupled with the drastic engine problems suffered by the Tigers at Le Mans, convinced Marcus and Ian (Des O'Dell had still not joined the team by that stage) that they should stay well clear of the Tour de France, at least in 1964. They were wise, no question, for above all the Tour demanded reliable cars. This was the year, for

instance, in which the entire team of 'works' AC Cobras retired with mechanical troubles, and when only one of the four Triumph Spitfires which I was managing made it to the end. Even that car had a leaking fuel tank by the last day.

Ian remembers that the development programme was fraught with problems, which included breaking Panhard rod mountings, engines overheating, and brakes giving problems too:

We developed the Tiger purely on a trial basis. 'Tiny' Lewis and I took the first one on a minor event in Italy, where we ran out of petrol, which sounds unrealistic. That was a Jim Ashworth special, where he had put an extra fuel tank in, and had got the gauge all wrong. It read two gallons or whatever when it was empty – but it read just the same when it had got 12 gallons in, which was all rather confusing...

Then we found it overheated, so we had to put a bigger radiator in. Then we found that the engine under-bonnet temperatures were too high, so we had to cut vents into the wings, then we found that the brakes didn't work, so we fitted Minilite wheels which did the trick...

Basically, of course, it was quite a good car, once we had semi-rally-developed it, far better than it had any right to be. Surprisingly there wasn't much Alpine experience, racing or rallying, which was much help. Most of the Tiger's problems were all inherent in the excessive amount of power and the heavy weight of the engine. Things like the axle tramp, which was quite severe and which would never have worried the Alpine, and the heavy understeer because of the motor, and the overheating – none of these things had cropped up, I assume, with the Alpine, which was a thoroughly well-developed, normal, Rootes Group car.

Early in the life of the 'works' Tiger, Rootes always liked to make a strong connection between them and the more affordable Hillman Imps. These two cars, on show in Rootes's own Devonshire House showrooms, had just completed the 1965 Monte Carlo rally.

Before the 'works' cars could be truly effective, they had to be developed and tested. AHP 294B was one of the early 'works' cars, looking distinctly 'provisional' at this stage, festooned with lamps and unfinished cooling slots in the wings. There's no substitute for mileage, though.

When the time came to introduce the Tiger to rallying there was no shortage of good drivers, for Rootes, somehow, had collected a fine team even though the Rapiers (and especially the Imps) were not winning cars. Not only Peter Harper, Peter Procter and Rosemary Smith were available, but Keith Ballisat always drove if his Shell motorsport commitments allowed it, 'Tiny' Lewis was not only a very good and patient test driver but a successful rally driver, while a young Andrew Cowan was also on his way up.

By September, development had progressed so far that a team of three new red Tigers – ADU 310B, ADU 311B and ADU 312B – had been completed. As was becoming the fashion in those days, all of them had left-hand-drive, for if most of a team car's work was going to be on the continent, it might as well have its wheel on the same side of the car as every other machine it would meet on public highways over there.

Geneva 1964 and Monte Carlo 1965 – A Good Start

When I saw three cars lined up for the start of the Geneva rally, it was obvious that they had been prepared in a hurry. It wasn't that they didn't look fast or purposeful, it was merely that they didn't have

Here is a sequence of three fascinating pictures of one car, on one event. Before they started the event, Peter Harper (right) and Ian Hall (left) look confident about their prospects in the 1965 Monte Carlo rally. It was to prove one of the most demanding Montes ever held.

the detail preparation 'sheen' of a big Healey, or even the gloss of a 'works' Rapier. The cooling holes in the wings were just that – no grilles to cover them, no flanges.

Strangely, it was 'Tiny' Lewis, Peter Riley and Rosemary Smith who were to drive the cars. The experienced team-leader, Peter Harper, was left at home (Why? Was it because he and co-driver Peter Procter had just won the Tour de France in a Ford Mustang), but why couldn't Keith Ballisat compete in a tarmac event which should have suited his skills ?

By this time the cars had Shelby-prepared engines (hopefully, these were bet-ter-prepared than the Le Mans units had been), along with close-ratio gearboxes, Salisbury-type axles (with which Des O'Dell was very familiar), and cast alloy Minilite wheels.

There were no Big Healeys running, so Marcus Chambers and Ian Hall could make no comparisons with their rivals, and as this was a handicap event which allowed smaller-engined cars to finish higher up the order than their performance really justified, there was not a lot to be learned, except about the new cars' reliability.

Although there were problems with clutches, and fan belts on the engines, the good news was that the Tigers started the

Even on the non-competitive sections there was usually deep, hard-packed, snow on the 1965 Monte. Peter Harper is resting at this moment while co-driver Ian Hall steers the 'works' Tiger towards the next check point. Note the five extra driving lamps, and the raised front suspension settings.

event with competition numbers 1,2, and 3 – which was good for local publicity – and all three cars finished, taking first, second and third places in the Over 2,500cc GT category.

O'Dell soon discovered the Tiger's overheating problems, and what dealing with Rootes bureaucracy was like:

I had several discussions with the slide-rule boffins, chaps who had never sat inside a competition car in their lives... Using one of the development cars, I would go for a run down the motorway and open it up to 120mph (192km/h), but within about six miles it would boil!

Anyway, I did some checks, and found that the air was passing through every-where but the radiator, so I instructed the engineers to put in more air ducts. Then I remembered that Aston Martin and Mercedes-Benz had suffered from similar problems, and they had cured them by altering the header tank layout...

This was the first of many references to Aston Martin which Des, an ex-Aston Martin racing mechanic, would make in the next few years.

Back in Britain, where high temperatures were not a problem in November, another new 'works' car – AHP 483B – was completed in time to be driven by one of Marcus Chambers' old chums, the Reverend Rupert Jones, in the RAC Rally. Front-line team drivers were sent out in

Throughout the 1965 Monte, the only 'dry-tarmac' test was on the short La Roquette test just north-west of Monte Carlo where the sports cars could at last show their pace. At the end of an amazing event, Car 107, driven by Peter Harper and Ian Hall, finished fourth overall, while their team-mates Andrew Cowan / Robin Turvey took 11th place.

Imps, which must have been a very pedestrian business. Rupert crashed the Tiger on the second day, so little was learned.

Then came the 1965 Monte Carlo, an event remembered by those who were involved in it (myself included) for the ferocity of the weather, the blizzard-like conditions, and the laws of sheer chance which governed whether a car would finish or not. Rootes, as often, seemed to find the funds to enter a fleet of cars – three Imps and two Tigers, one of them (ADU 312B) for Peter Harper/Ian Hall, the other (AHP 295B) for Andrew Cowan/Robin Turvey.

Conditions between St Claude (north of Geneva) and Monte Carlo were so awful that only thirty-five of the 276 starters reached the Mediterranean, with the last numbers suffering much more than the early ones. Andrew Cowan was on No. 103, and Peter Harper was on No. 107, so it was a miracle that they managed to blast their way through the drifts.

History relates that Timo Makinen's Mini-Cooper S won the event – but Peter Harper completed one of his legendary balancing acts to thread the Tiger delicately into fourth place overall, the Tiger being the first conventional (i.e. front engine/rear-drive) car to finish. Andrew Cowan, not yet the master of such a powerful car, plugged on to take eleventh place.

1965 Alpine – High Tide, Low Tide

After the euphoria created by the Monte, the Tiger then battled through a series of highs and lows.

The Tiger entries in the Tulip rally (for Peter Harper and Peter Riley) were both forced to retire, when they encountered freak snow storms in Switzerland (in May, for goodness sake!). Climbing long and steep passes without spiked tyres (which, naturally, the Rootes service crew was not

carrying) was impossible for this ultra-powerful car, so they both ran out of time.

What annoyed everyone about the Tulip was that here was an event which really ought to have been settled by brute performance on speed hill climbs and sprints, with the Morley Twins' 'works' Austin-Healey 3000 as the main opposition – and the weather had negated everything.

Nor was there any more luck, for Andrew Cowan, on the Scottish rally, where his Tiger objected to all the rough stages and gradually battered its way to destruction. It did not help that at one stage the Tiger had lost its oil through a leak, and that Cowan had topped up the engine with the wrong type of oil (vegetable instead of mineral) so terminal engine failure was imminent even before the badly crumpled car was retired. Team boss Marcus Chambers was not best pleased.

John Gott (by then the Chief Constable of Northamptonshire) then borrowed the ex-Cowan Monte car to attack the International Police rally in May, and was delighted to win it outright, but unhappily for Rootes there was no commercial spin-off from this, as there was really little future for small two-seater sports cars, however fast, in British police fleets!

Then came the French Alpine, where the still-developing Tigers were expecting a head-to-head fight against the 'works' big Healeys. Because it was held in high summer, on tarmac roads, and without stupid handicaps to get in the way, this ought to have been the prize fight to end them all.

And so it was. Rootes entered three Tigers – all by now sporting the forward facing bonnet air scoop which was intended (and successfully, as it transpired) to reduce engine bay temperatures. Peter Harper, Tiny Lewis and Peter Riley should have been driving, but Riley had to drop out at the last moment, which meant that

Peter Harper/Ian Hall on the Tulip rally of 1965, at the Nurburgring test. Normal weather for May in Europe, of course but...

...there was a freak snow storm in France and Switzerland only hours later, which had the entire rally floundering – and spiked tyres were not available to most crews. Was it any wonder that the Tigers did not figure in the results?

Three significant personalities in the Rootes 'works' team in the mid 1960s. Marcus Chambers (in glasses) discusses a route card problem with his assistant Ian Hall (in light shirt) and Don Barrow (co-driver) before the 1965 Alpine rally.

Assistant Competitions Manager Ian Hall finally got a chance to drive, instead of co-driving.

The event started from Marseilles in the evening, and all went well until the following morning, when Ian Hall (driving ADU 311B) hit a barrier on the descent of the Col d'Allos, which put him out of the event. Ian later told me that a lack of pratice on the stage got the better of him, and that he could see the accident approaching well before it actually happened.

Later Tiny Lewis's car (which had already suffered a fire connected with his brakes) crashed and was out of the event, which left Peter Harper and his co-driver Mike Hughes to carry on the battle.

At the end of the first leg, the Tiger was third behind a Porsche 904 (this was really a racing car) and the Morley twins' Austin-Healey. On the second leg, though, Buchet's Porsche crashed, while the Austin-Healey suffered delays when the engine shredded its fan belt, so by the time only thirty-nine of the original ninety-three starters began the final section – from Grenoble back to the Mediterranean – Harper's Tiger was leading the entire event.

In the last eighteen hours, all went well for the Tiger, which remained unpenalized on the road, and was hailed as outright victor when it reached Monaco. Then the trouble started. Post-event scrutiny, and a stripped Ford V8 engine, revealed that the Tiger's engine was fitted with non-standard – actually undersized – valves in the cylinder head, whereupon the French stewards disqualified the car from the event, handing victory to Rene Trautmann's Lancia Flavia Zagato instead.

Rootes management, which had already started the celebrations, was aghast, and no amount of special pleading could reverse the stewards' decision. Rootes's own statement, issued later, did not clear up the puzzle:

> By fitting smaller valves to the Tiger, we certainly did not gain any advantage in performance, and this was only done to bring the rally car specification into line with that of current models...

Nothing could hide the fact that Rootes had boobed in the biggest possible way, either by making homologation mistakes in the first place (Marcus Chambers thinks the early Shelby-built race engines had been used for measurement purposes), or by preparing the wrong engines for the Alpine cars.

The homologation rules were quite clear – quoted valve sizes could not be changed – which made the press statement naive. As I later wrote, for Peter Garnier's 'The Sport' column in *Autocar*:

> Several of the less well-informed publications seemed to think that 'they [Rootes]

wuz robbed'.

But rules are rules, and there can be no excuse for fitting non-homologated items to a factory car, even if they are now normally fitted parts.

None the less it is a great pity that this should deprive Peter Harper of the only Coupe des Alpes won by a Grand Touring car, and of the Tiger's first victory over the ageing Healey 3000.

Much heat and light was generated at the time, but in later years most of the personalities involved, not least Marcus Chambers and mechanic (later Competitions Manager) Des O'Dell, both admitted repeatedly that they had made an honest mistake.

As someone who actually took part in the event (in one of the 'works' Spitfires, which went on to win the Prototype Category), I believe the Harper/Tiger performance is still under-estimated. This was a ferociously fast event, with extremely demanding average speeds, and Harper's performance in not only defeating the cream of Europe's drivers, but meeting that schedule to finish unpenalized on the road sections, was quite amazing.

It is also worth pointing out that the 'illegal' engine changes had certainly not improved the Tiger's performance, for this was never an objective. Even with the racing-type tyres used on the Alpine it was already a car with more power than traction, and brakes which always let the side down if used long enough and hard enough!

In connection with this farrago, Ian Hall thinks that the department's efforts were all being stretched too far at the time:

> We were always short of money – I was for ever dreaming up events which we ought to do, but there was never the money to do them.

Now here's an oddity – two co-drivers in the same rally car. When a nominated driver could not take part in the event, Ian Hall took the wheel of this 'works' Tiger for the 1965 Alpine rally, with Don Barrow as his co-driver. This was the start from Marseille...

...and this was a few hours later, in the French Alps, just before the Tiger went off the road, due to braking problems, on the Col d'Allos. Note the large forward facing scoop which the Tigers used at this stage to channel cool air straight into the carburettors of the highly-tuned V8 engines.

183

In the end I became rather out of sorts with the Tiger. We used to run too many cars, given our budget and our resources. If you'd got, say, two Tigers and three Imps in a rally, the amount of spares you need-ed to carry for those two models was quite ridiculous. Nothing – nothing – except spot lamps, was common to both.

In retrospect, it wasn't clever to enter Tigers and Imps on the same events. I think I was the person who shouted loud-est against that, and I was very unpopular for that, because I think everyone else felt that both cars were on the verge of a breakthrough all the time.

1965 and 1966 – More Frustration

The Alpine fiasco quite knocked the stuff-ing out of the department, and although the Tiger's reputation did not suffer, team morale certainly did. There were no more highlights during 1965, especially in the RAC rally, where both cars retired at a very early stage.

The next blow, also suffered by BMC and Triumph, was that the homologation regu-lations changed significantly at the end of 1966. One consequence of this was that there were no longer any allowances to change a GT or sports car's body work – and, at a stroke, the Tigers could no longer use cooling vents in the side of the front wings, nor could they use the long fresh-air scoops in the bonnet panels.

Although few Tiger fanatics would admit it at the time, this meant that the 1966 cars were not nearly as good as they had been in 1965, for they could no longer keep their engines as cool as before. Engineers like Des O'Dell were thoroughly frustrated, for what they could achieve was no longer allowed, and Rootes was not about to stray to the wrong side of the homologation rules again.

Because the new rules applied to the Monte Carlo rally (the organisers were determined to favour standard, showroom specification saloons, and some said this was to favour the French Citroens) the 'works' Tigers were never likely to be fight-ing for a victory, but because this was still such a high-profile event, two were entered for Andrew Cowan and Peter Harper to drive.

Cowan's rally lasted only into the second day, when he crashed on icy roads near Boulogne, while Peter Harper/Ian Hall had to retire after the engine fan blades some-how mangled the radiator, causing all the water to leak out.

Scratch two Tigers.

Then came the Tulip rally, where the Tigers had suffered so badly in freak snow in 1965. In 1966, though, weather condi-tions were spring-like all the way down from Holland to Switzerland, and back. This year, praise be, there were no handi-caps either, so the fastest car would win the event.

Although the 'works' Austin-Healey 3000s had been withdrawn from rallying – the homologation changes had hit them too hard for them to still be competitive – Rootes thought the Tiger ideal for the job. This time Peter Harper took Robin Turvey as his co-driver (Ian Hall was concentrat-ing on team management this time), and he used a newly-built 1966 specification car, FRW 668C.

Like all the 'works' Tigers, this was a left-hand-drive car – because of the cars' intended use in Continental Europe, not because right-hand-drive cars were not available, as one other Tiger author has suggested – and it was running in the lat-est corporate blue colour, as ever with a hardtop.

Hillclimbs, speed tests and special stages sorted out the brave from the 'holi-

For 1966 the regulations of rallying had changed yet again, banning extra scoops and holes. Although the registration number – ADU 311B – was familiar, this was a different shell from 1965. Peter Harper and Ian Hall ready to start the Acropolis rally of 1966.

day-makers'. Apart from the Tiger's locking steering column adjustment regularly coming loose, which must have made life interesting for Peter at times, the Tiger looked faster and more stable than ever before.

Throughout the event, only four cars looked like winning outright – Rauno Aaltonen's Mini-Cooper S, Vic Elford's Lotus Cortina and W .Gass's Porsche 911 being Harper's obvious rivals – and in the end the Tiger not only won the entire GT category, but finished third overall. The total times taken over all the tests were interesting :

1	Aaltonen (Mini-Cooper S)	3880.5 sec
2	Elford (Ford Lotus-Cortina)	3925.4 sec
3	P. Harper (Sunbeam Tiger)	3962.5 sec

Peter, in other words, had finished eighty-two seconds adrift, in a total of about sixty-five minutes of flat-out motoring. Close, but not quite close enough.

Even so, it was all very encouraging. Against all the odds, however, Rootes then entered a 'works' Tiger for the Greek Acropolis rally, where it joined a couple of Imps. Following the demise of the Spa–Sofia–Liège Marathon, the Acropolis rally was now agreed to be the fastest, roughest and most demanding rally in the European calendar.

This particular Tiger was registered ADU 311B, though this was a very different machine from the ADU 311B which had been used in 1964 and 1965. Shorn of its earlier scoops and slots, I am sure that it had a new body shell for the occasion (it was blue, rather than its earlier red, too), and to cope with the Acropolis's rocks, it was also equipped with a massive sump shield.

At the end of a hot and dusty event (the attraction of the Acropolis, everyone used to say at the time, was that it started and finished in Athens, with all the serious teams staying at beach hotels where they could top-up their suntans, and their swimming) the good news was that the Tiger jolted, banged and scraped its way around Greece to win the GT Category (and finished seventh overall).

The bad news, though, was that this proved what Triumph had concluded only two years earlier – that low-slung sports cars and modern rough-stage rallies simply didn't go together any more. Ian Hall, whose pictures of this event show driver, co-driver and car looking progressively more shattered as the event progressed, was very clear:

Even after Rootes had decided to retire the Tiger from tough rough-road events, Peter Harper and Robin Turvey took a very hard-working 'works' rally car, ADU 311B, on the British Gulf London Marathon. It was an event where pace counted just as much as durability. He was unlucky – first crashing off the road on a stage in Yorkshire, then losing a wheel and having to retire.

I felt that that particular Acropolis was among the hardest rallies that I personally have ever done, and I think Harper agreed. At the end of it we were utterly exhausted it was particularly hot and dusty.

The Tiger got very hot in the cockpit. Towards the end of the event we were crashing and banging around in this four-and-a-quarter-litre monster, working like hell, and scraping into controls with about thirty seconds in hand, while that nice Swede, Ove Andersson, came touring in in a Lancia Fulvia 1300, not even an HF, relaxed and quiet, with minutes in hand.

This p****d me off, frankly, and I felt that the Tiger had just had it – it was just an out of date leviathan.

I don't think we needed any more power, we needed a modern chassis with more traction, better braking, bigger wheels and maybe a longer wheelbase – in other words the car was really operating beyond its time span.

This, mark you, was not an opinion made a few minutes after an exhausted Hall had peeled himself out of the car in Athens, but many years later, when he had had time to generate final opinions.

What is known, for sure, is that Marcus Chambers soon came to terms with the fact that the Tiger was now a rally car out of its time. Five or more years earlier, when there were plenty of tarmac-only rallies around, and when the competition against the Austin-Healeys could have been truly stimulating, there would have been a point in pushing onwards, perhaps even using the Tiger II, but not in 1966.

One is reminded irresistibly of what was stated, defiantly, in *Sunset Boulevard*: 'It wasn't the stars who got too big, but the movies which got too small.' You could say the same about the Tiger. Another time, another place…

10 Today's Alpines and Tigers – Keeping Them Fit and Healthy

In the mid-1970s the reputations of Alpines and Tigers were still low. Although the 'classic' movement was developing fast, all over the world, the Rootes sports cars seemed to have been forgotten by enthusiasts aiming to buy flashier and more obvious machines.

But to quote an oft-used aphorism which originated in the USA (where the vast majority of these cars were originally sold) – that was then and this is now. Which, being loosely translated, means that Alpines and Tigers are once again seen as the sturdy, capable and nicely-styled sports cars which they always were.

More Alpines and Tigers are now in use than ten years ago, and the gradual loss of cars due to terminal corrosion seems to have been halted. This is not only because the cars are more popular (need I use the word 'collectible'?) than before, but because more and more parts (some remanufactured) have become available to put them right.

Where To Find Today's Alpines and Tigers?

Although detail figures are no longer available, it is certain that at least 80 per cent of all the Alpines produced were originally sold overseas. Many of them went to North America (the USA and Canada – one must never forget Canada, even though cars in that nation have a hard time because of the bitterly cold and snowy winters), but a sizeable number went to strong Rootes markets such as Australia and New Zealand, South Africa, and other fast-disappearing 'Empire' territories.

More detailed delivery statistics are available for the Tiger project. I have seen figures which suggest that only 812 of the 7,083 cars produced – that is only 11 per cent – were ever sold in Britain as new cars, and that no fewer than 5,681 cars (or 80 per cent, which ties in neatly with Alpine estimates) were sold in the North American continent between 1964 and 1968.

Because of the way these cars were designed, as they got old their all-steel monocoques tended to rust away, so anyone contemplating buying a car in the 1990s needs to know that it has either been totally, lovingly and expertly maintained and restored – or that it has spent its life in one of the world's 'dry' climates.

A few years ago it was fashionable – and easy – to buy a nearly rust-free British sports car which had been sold and used in a rust-free zone such as the southern states of the USA, or (in smaller numbers) from parts of Australia where the sun never seems to stop shining.

Nowadays it may still be fashionable, but prices have rocketed as owners living in those parts of the world come to realise the worth of their previously discarded and unloved machines. There's no doubt, however, that there has been a general movement of Alpines and Tigers away from the USA (where they are not thought to be as desirable as some other cars also available in big numbers), back to the UK.

Best Buys? A Difficult Choice

This is the point at which an author knows he is going to make new friends – and lose others. Whether in print, or when talking to a gathering of club enthusiasts, he is inevitably asked to name his favourite model. Oh dear!

Having driven, extensively in most cases, almost every model of the Alpine and Tiger (I never laid hands on a Tiger II, alas), I can see the attractions and letdowns of all of them. I hoped I could get

away with suggesting that as long as it had wire spoke wheels and an overdrive, then I would be happy, but I was told that this was a cop-out. However, if you insist...

Maybe it tells you a lot about me, and the number of years that I have been owning, enjoying and driving cars, but I would want to make sure all the 'essential' extras such as the heater, the overdrive and the wire spoke wheels were fitted, and I need to have a hardtop model. At least I would know that the top could be removed, and stowed, during the summer months.

Of all the Alpines, from the finned generation I would certainly choose an Alpine II, because it was that slightly better developed than the Alpine I, with a better driving position, a little more torque, and

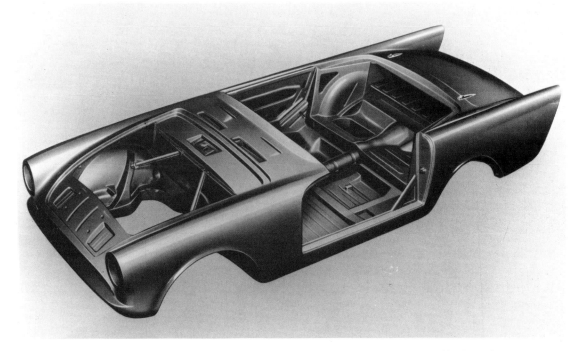

This retouched factory shot shows the basic construction of the Alpine's body shell. Nowadays it isn't easy to find panels (new or refurbished) to help the restoration of rusty old examples to as-new condition. Because every panel was steel, in the UK, at least, rust is a serious problem; for rust-free examples, try the southern states of the USA, or Australia, where, remarkably, original machinery survives.

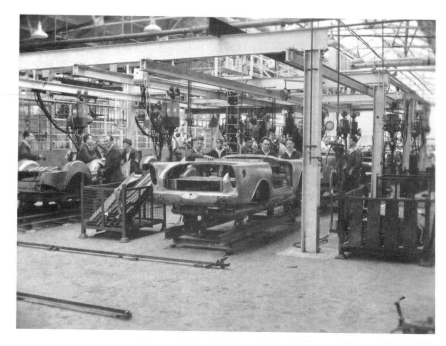

This is how early Alpines were welded together in 1959 – the problem today is that the sub-assemblies were welded together, which means that you can't strip out the structure to start a rebuild.

more practical details like the full-length window glass support in the doors. Incidentally, I'd like to have a brake servo fitted, even though such a piece of kit was not standard at the time when the car was in production.

I'm sorry to say that I wouldn't choose an Alpine III because although I like the way the new boot/petrol tank/spare wheel packaging was carried out, I don't find the styling match between the angular hardtop and the befinned tail quite to my liking.

Of the later models, I would choose the last of all, the Alpine V, complete with its most powerful 1,725cc engine (even though it isn't as easy to set and tune Zenith-Stromberg carburettors), and the all-synchromesh gearbox.

Tigers? Well, in the UK I have little choice, because Tiger IIs are still as rare as wooden rocking horse droppings/hen's teeth/politicians who admit that they were wrong/traffic policemen who make allowances (strike out those you don't approve of!).

Perversely, though, I'm going to choose the Tiger II, even if I have to travel to the USA (never, repeat never, buy a car unless you have seen it yourself) to find a car, inspect it, and arrange for transportation to the UK. And yes, I admit it – when I have it back in the UK I will arrange for the doubtless difficult and expensive conversion to right-hand-drive.

[Believe me, I've owned left-hand-drive cars, which were exclusive but, on crowded British roads, really no fun to drive]

On the whole, too, I think I would want whatever Tiger I chose, to be mechanically standard. OK, so the Ford V8 engine is very tuneable, the gearbox is supposed to be able to withstand extra torque from a tuned-up engine, and if the Salisbury back axle can deal with Jaguar torque it ought to be able to handle whatever Uncle Henry throws at it, but somehow I've always liked my cars to be the way their makers sold them.

How important is originality to you? Many latter-day owners have fitted chunkier wheels (especially to Tigers like this example) to give their cars more special appeal.

After Purchase, What To Look For, and What To Do

A few years ago, *Classic Cars* asked me to survey the market in 'classic' Alpines, and the following is a summary of what I concluded at the time. That feature, published in June 1991, was created with the enthusiastic help of the then-Chairman of the Sunbeam Alpine Owners Club, Paul Norton, so it was as authentic as possible. Unless I make it clear below, every remark also applies to Tigers as well.

Paul, incidentally, was no figurehead Chairman, as I discovered on my visit to see him. Not only was he using an Alpine V for regular, day-to-day, transport in the British home counties, but he was restoring an Alpine II, from the monocoque upwards, in every spare hour that he could find.

Paul started by cautioning me, and anyone who read the feature, that because the majority of all body/monocoque panels, skin panels or structural pressings, were obsolete, it was always going to be extremely difficult to restore a badly rotted car. If the budget was available, of course, anything was possible, but the enthusiast would need to be an accomplished welder/panel- beater (or have a friend or colleague who was) to make a rebuild practical.

In many cases, parts supply is impossible, not only because most Alpines were already more than thirty years old when the first edition of this book was being written, but because the Rootes Group no longer exists. The proportion of service support provided by Chrysler United Kingdom after it came into existence in 1970 was soon eliminated by Peugeot when it took over the business in 1978. That was many years ago, and things rapidly got worse.

In addition, when you go out looking for a car (or start to contemplate rebuilding an Alpine/Tiger you already own), consider the following.

Now there's a novelty! If you want to carry more than you can squeeze into an Alpine, why not make a two-wheel trailer out of the back end of another Alpine?

Structure

Like many other Pressed Steel Co.-inspired monocoques of the period, the shell was riddled with potential rust-traps, and places where muck and salt spray can settle and remain, undisturbed.

First of all, you should check that the shell still feels solid, that the doors open and close smoothly without snagging the pillars, and the windscreen surround feels secure. This will give you a feel for the general condition. If the doors jam or don't hang properly, this could be an indication that the scuttle/bulkhead from which they hang is rotting away (or has distorted), or that the floor/sills have suffered badly from rot and may have started to wilt.

Look at the jacking points, front and rear, which are under the bumpers and are welded to the front and rear 'chassis legs'. These may creak badly when used, or may already have crumbled away. This symptom, and the fact that the door shut line tolerances may disappear when a car is jacked up, may mean that the rest of the shell is rusting badly and no longer be rigid enough to get past even a tolerant MoT tester.

Other places to look should be the sills (there are three pressings involved - inner, central and outer), the ends of the cruciform crossmember pressings (in spite of their bulk, they certainly rot out at the extremities) and the front hangers/mounting brackets for the rear leaf springs.

Rot in the front bulkhead is usually very difficult to eradicate. Door hinge mounts on SI/SII can suffer badly (though on later models, after a redesign, things improved a lot). On top of this bulkhead, look for signs of 'dimpling' ahead of the windscreen. Rust has often started following water ingress under the double skinning in this part of the shell.

There are serious corrosion possibilities on the inner wheelarches at front *and* rear, particularly behind the front wheels on the wheelarch closing panel, and also where the two-piece inner rear arches are joined together.

Once the inner arches start to rot, of course, the skin panels are sure to follow. Not only that, but if either inner arch lets water through rust holes, this then finds its way into the sills themselves, and that can be both complicated and expensive to repair.

Other 'look for' points include the doors themselves, which seem to be rot-prone just about everywhere, but especially along the front and bottom panels, the rear-base of the Series III–V optional hardtops (but not the earlier SI/SII hard-tops, which were aluminium pressings) and the screen surround of Series III–V models.

The rear of the shell is effectively jointed to the floor behind and below the door openings, and this joint is by no means as strong as the rest of the car. Rusting in this area usually means big expense, a complete strip-out, and major surgery to get the shell back to its original strength.

Some cars, too, suffer from badly rotted floor panels, and rot in the strengthening panels inside the cockpit and close to the doors and sills. Rusting can also occur around the headlamp openings (this is a common failing on some of the Alpine's British sports car rivals).

The fact that many Alpines have always had notoriously oil-leaky engines (the Rootes unit used in this car was notorious for this service problem, which was never truly solved) may even have helped to pre-serve the engine bay panels, the bulkhead and the underside of the footwells and transmission tunnel, but don't make any assumptions! In any case, the Alpine rarely seems to suffer from terminal rot in the 'chassis legs' (which were very sturdily constructed and engineered) or in the scuttle.

Many body panels, no longer available from factory sources, have been remanufactured – the all important wings, sills and repair sections among them.

Tiger: Because of the loads imposed on it by the Panhard rod in a hard-driven Tiger, look very carefully at the condition of the mounting bracket on the inner side of the chassis leg. Reinforcement or double-skin repair may be necessary, and is advisable.

Engines

This Rootes engine is solid, reliable, unexciting – and therefore straightforward to maintain, restore and repair. It always had something of a reputation for leaking oil (rather than burning it). Most leaks come from around the edges of the valvegear inspection cover, and from the other various gasket joints. Some experts blame cost-cutting, and the use of too-thin gaskets, for which there is no obvious permanent cure.

In old age, wear occurs at the crankshaft thrust bearing (you can identify this by dipping the clutch at idling speeds, when the engine may stall), but valvegear wear is usually limited to valve guides, seals and tappets. In old age, engines become rattly (not even the new ones were totally refined) and in many cases the carburettors, particularly twin-carb installations, will be out of adjustment.

Over the years many engines have been made non-standard by previous owners (usually they are looking for more power, or just to customize their units). However, if

The clue to this engine installation is the magic word 'Holbay' on the engine cover. Holbay developed the twin-Weber engine installation for the later Sunbeam Rapier H120, and this is a very similar Alpine installation. Originality doesn't matter to Alpine enthusiasts who would rather have a much more powerful example.

you know what is fitted, there are experts in the Club who can advise on what to do to revert to standard.

The five-bearing 1,725cc engines are the smoothest of all, but all types should be good for well over 100,000 miles before any major work is required.

The aluminium cylinder heads may have corroded internally without any owner realising this, especially if the wrong type of coolant, without inhibitors, has been used. Happily, hundreds of thousands of such heads were manufactured, and there is no problem in finding, using and fitting 1970s-type heads.

All types of replacement carburettors – fixed-jet or constant-vacuum are available.

Tiger : The engines and gearboxes, being stressed for use in heavier cars, and designed in the sure and certain knowledge that they would be neglected by most American owners, have a reputation for lasting almost indefinitely. Just so long as you keep changing the oil, adjusting the valvegear, and telling the engine you love it at regular intervals, it should certainly outlast the rest of the car.

Parts supply, too, is no problem.

One of the Tiger's failings, due to the

Now is this sacrilege or what? What started out as a Sunbeam Alpine – not even a Tiger – has ended up in the mid-1990s with a fuel-injected Ford V6. It probably has more power than a standard Tiger I, but not as much as a Tiger II. Few Alpine owners want to go this far.

way the engine completely filled the bonnet, was that it tended to overheat in slow-moving traffic. For that reason, the radiator may have had a hard time, and you should always check this out before buying. Replacement radiators of a higher-than-normal performance are available.

Transmissions

There were two different types of gearbox used in Alpines – from late 1964 an all-synchromesh type was standard across Rootes's medium-size car range – and over the years there were several different sets of internal ratios. The available literature (and this book) makes all this clear. However, since the cars went out of production, and particularly in the unfashionable period, many Alpines have been rendered non-standard for their type, merely to keep them going.

Both gearboxes are ruggedly simple designs (they share a number of internal, rotating, components), and should retain their relatively precise change into old age. Naturally the synchromesh wears away after many years, but complete rebuilds are always possible. The Club will advise on specialists.

Most (but not all) Alpines have Laycock overdrives. As they get old, many of these stop working, not because anything is broken, but because the control mechanisms have ceased to function. Unless the actual oil inside the unit is filthy (and has therefore had a chance to clog up the control mechanisms and valves) most of the problems are electrical – particularly failed solenoids.

All Laycock overdrives can be rebuilt by experts, but this is not a job for DIY enthusiasts to tackle, unless they have previous experience and have access to the special fixtures and knowledge involved.

There may be some oil leaks between gearbox and overdrive, and if a total restoration is being carried out it is certainly worth renewing every gasket and seal, and of course to treat the entire transmission to a thorough clean out, and a refill with fresh, modern, oil of the correct type.

Apart from checking that the correct ratio is fitted, there should be no major problem with the rear axles.

Tiger : As with the engine, the Ford-USA manual gearbox was designed for much more severe usage than it ever got in the Tiger. At worst, you may have to have it rebuilt with new synchro rings, and at the same time make sure that there is no play in the prop-shaft universal joints, or in the half-shafts inside the Salisbury axle.

Running Gear

The front crossmember is a massive pressing, and unless it has ever been involved in an accident (when some of the brackets may have been distorted) it should rarely need more than a clean, a through brushing out to get rid of all muck and deposits, followed by a repaint, to bring it back to 'as-new' condition.

The front suspension itself may be suffering from badly worn upper or lower-ball-joints in the vertical links, but replacements and all related details are available. Bearings, pivots and bushes in the wishbones seem to last very well (this was a very sturdy design, remember, intended for use under heavier cars than the Alpine, in worse conditions) but earlier types need regular lubrication. Your handbook will give details of the schedule, and of what lubricants to use. From the start of Series IV assembly, virtually all greasing points were eliminated.

Front dampers (shock absorbers) though not too large in physical size, seem to keep their settings over long periods, though even the nominal settings can seem quite soft to those owners coming to the Alpine from, say, a Triumph TR or an Austin-Healey.

The easy way to make an Alpine handle better than standard – but an easy way, also, to destroy the ride comfort – is to have the dampers uprated with stiffer settings, and to increase the anti-roll bar diameter.

At the rear end, check that the rear springs have not sagged. Ideally these should be flat, or very slightly convex, when the car is stationery and unladen – the nominal figures are published in the Manuals. Rear dampers on earlier cars are lever-arm types, which may need rebuilding, or preferably renewing completely. Later models (SIII–SV) have telescopic rear dampers, which seem to do a better long-term job.

The steering box was never inch-accurate even when new, and it will certainly have worn over the years, but this recirculating ball type can be rebuilt, and completely reconditioned boxes are available (but they are costly). As with the related suspension, most steering gear wear comes in the ball joints of the linkage, but replacements are available.

On earlier Alpines (SI to SIII) it is vitally important that you should follow greasing and lubrication recommendations to preserve the linkage, especially as some nipples are well hidden away when the engine is in place, and with years of grime scattered around.

The front disc/rear drum brake system is simple of its kind, and Girling still stocks seals and other replacement parts for this car (for the same basic set-up was used on several other cars, not only built by Rootes). The front discs suffer from scoring and ridging after heavy use, which also means that front pads then tend to wear out quite persistently, though rear drums and shoes seem to last for at least 50,000 miles at a time.

Discs can be skimmed (but don't let the disc then get too thin – no bacon slicers, please!), and replacement discs are also available. Rear drums seem to go on for ever.

Brake servos (standard on SIII–SV models, optional on earlier types) may need rebuilding, but service kits are still available from Girling. This job is best left to an expert.

Incidentally, if there seems to be a persistent loss of brake fluid, and external leaks are not obvious, the fluid might be getting into the servo chamber itself. You should soon spot this, because when the fluid then eventually passes back to the inlet manifold (along the vacuum pipe) and gets burnt in the engine, it will produce rather alarming white smoke in the car's exhaust.

Tiger: As you might expect, the rack-and-pinion steering system has quite a hard life. It is intrinsically much more accurate than the recirculating ball system of the Alpine, but there will eventually be wear in the track rod ends. Factory sources have long since been abandoned, but the Club reports that replacements from the ubiquitous Morris Minor do a good job.

Electrics and Interiors

The battery lives in a pressed steel box in the floor behind the seats: this sometimes rots away, due not only to rusting but also because there might have been some battery acid spillage over time.

Lucas supplies newly-manufactured replacement parts for many British cars, including these Alpines, and the Club will certainly advise which are the difficult-to-source components. Remember that on Series V cars only, an alternator replaced the DC dynamo (generator) of earlier cars, and was fitted with a separate control box.

At restoration time, be sure that you only use negative-earth electrical components for a negative-earth installation, and vice versa. Failure to notice which is which (handbooks advise) could lead to a lot of burnt-out bits, aggravation, heartache, and a furious bank manager.

If the Alpine has been kept as a regularly-used car, the electrical system should give you little on-going trouble. Storage, allied to damp getting into the starter and dynamo or alternator, can lead to all manner of problems.

Instruments were shared with several other Rootes cars of the period – notably Rapiers and Humber Sceptres – but when picking up replacement instruments such as speedometers at auto-jumbles, always make sure that they are properly matched to the axle ratio and the mph/1,000rpm figures of your own Alpine. Not only are there 'overdrive' and 'non-overdrive' ratios to be considered, but different axle ratios with different models, while the ratios on Rapiers and Sceptres are different again.

When it comes to sourcing new carpets and trim panels, you should certainly consult Club experts, as there have been no factory-supplied parts for many years. Good-quality replica parts are now on the market. One big problem (shared with other open-top cars) is that interiors may have got thoroughly wet from time to time, not only because they may have run without soft-tops erected, but because corrosion may have allowed water to enter through front and rear bulkheads, or around the floor pan.

Replacement soft tops are readily available, at various prices depending on the quality and material you are prepared to settle for.

Tiger: Because the Tiger's battery lived in a different pocket compared with the Alpine (on the boot floor), that is one less corrosion problem to worry about, though of course there is still the chance of acid spillage onto the boot panel – which you will not notice unless you look for it, as the battery has a cover in normal use.

Buying A Car – a Warning

Even though these are great cars to own and use, please don't rush into buying one in the hope of turning it into a financial 'investment'. Those days, if they ever really existed, have now gone with the frenetic Eighties, and I think it is highly unlikely that sports car values will ever rise fast enough to make it worth 'investing' in them instead of in the stock market.

There are two obvious caveats. Unless you like half-breeds, don't buy an Alpine unless you are sure that it is an honest and original machine. I see little merit in buying an Alpine I with a 1,725cc engine, or even less merit in buying a later model car with early-model features.

I also happen to think that heavily customized cars, particularly those which have had engine transplants, are a waste of time and money. The market for them is very small, and frankly I do not see the added value either.

Finally, if you are out shopping for a Tiger, be sure that you find a genuine car, for several very ambitious transplant jobs have been carried out on standard Alpines – and in some cases Tigers have been re-shelled with modified versions of the easier-to-find Alpine shell which are similar, but *not* the same.

Join the Club!

To get the most out of your Alpines and Tigers, I recommend that you join the one-make club which concentrates on these cars. In Britain, in fact, there is a club for the Alpines, and an entirely separate club for the Tigers, and if you join that appropriate to your car, you will immediately gain access to the specialists and spares suppliers which will help you keep your car on the road.

When the first Edition of this book went to press in 1996, the two contacts were:

The Sunbeam Alpine Owners Club,
Membership Secretary,
Simon Edwards
31 Ingreway
Harold Park
ESSEX RM3 0BM
Tel : 01708 372306

The Sunbeam Tiger Owners Club,
Membership Secretary,
Brian Postle,
Beechwood,
8 Villa Real Estate,
Consett,
CO. DURHAM DH8 6BJ
Tel : 01207-508296.

Alpine and Tiger owners love to get together at club gatherings – to swap stories, to hunt for parts, to compete against each other, or just to enjoy themselves.

Appendix: The Chrysler Connection

In 1964 Rootes needed a saviour, while Chrysler needed an *entrée* to the British market, and to boost its presence in Europe. When the two Groups got together in the spring, the rationale was as simple as that. At any other time, and in any other place, there might never have been a deal.

Not that Rootes was a novice in setting up merger negotiations. Although Chrysler took a stake in the Rootes Group in 1964, the British company had already flirted with several other companies before then. Talks had been held, for instance, with Standard-Triumph in the mid-1950s, but these foundered in 1957 when Standard saw Rootes wanting too many of the managerial spoils. Then, as later, the Rootes family was never short of megalomania.

Over the years Rootes had often needed outside finance to help it fund its vigorous new model programme (the Prudential Assurance Company provided a lot of help), but in hindsight the Group was never sufficiently capitalized. Massive expansion to fund the Hillman Imp project at Linwood, near Glasgow, could only be tackled by taking out a big loan from the British Government.

All might have been well if bloody-minded unions had not precipitated a thirteen week strike at one of its London-based subsidiaries (British & Light Steel Pressings) in September 1961, which eventually crippled the entire group, and led to a loss of £2 million for the 1961–1962 financial year.

Even so, although Rootes lost money again in 1962–1963, company spokesmen put this down to the expense of launching the Imp, so when Lord Rootes suddenly announced that he had agreed to a financing deal with Chrysler of Detroit, this caused a sensation.

As the American motoring authority, Richard Langworth, later wrote:

> Lord Rootes had personally instituted the Chrysler deal, and he had great hopes for it in 1964. In that year, we must remember, it looked as though he'd made a wise decision. Chrysler was prosperous, highly profitable and needed entry to the European Economic Community. So indeed did Ryton [Rootes].'

Chrysler, in fact, had been founded by Walter P. Chrysler as recently as 1924. Chrysler himself had started life in the Union Pacific railway company, moved into Buick in 1906, eventually became President of that company, then moved to rescue Maxwell, which soon gave rise to the Chrysler marque.

By the 1960s Chrysler himself had been dead for some years, but the Corporation had diversified, and become the third biggest player in Detroit, behind General Motors and Ford. Along the way it had taken control of the Simca business in

France, and by 1963 was making more than a million cars – 500,000 Plymouths, 450,000 Dodges and 130,000 Chryslers – in a year.

Chrysler chief executive, Lynn Townsend, was ambitious, saw what GM (with Vauxhall and Opel) and Ford (with manufacturing plants in Britain and Germany) had already achieved, and determined to follow suit.

The Rootes family has always refused to open its heart about the past, even in retrospect, so we do not know if Lord Rootes had already been approached by other companies before first talking to Chrysler. We *do* know that it was Chrysler who made the first moves, in March 1964, that several meetings and much airline travel was needed before agreement was reached, and that the deal was clinched on 4 June 1964.

At that stage, Chrysler agreed to pay £12.3 million for a large stake, but not a controlling interest, in Rootes. For this investment, Chrysler got 30 per cent of the Ordinary (voting) and 50 per cent of the A Ordinary (non-voting) share capital. At the same time Chrysler pledged to the British government that it would not seek to gain control against its wishes.

Three Chrysler directors joined the Rootes board (strangely, Lynn Townsend was not among them), and although the American company did not have immediate control it was clear that it always exercised a great deal of influence on policy in the next few years. Its stake was increased by the sale of the British Dodge business to Rootes in the following year.

It may have been significant that Lord Rootes was already mortally ill at this time (though this was never publicized), and that he sold out rather than letting control of his company pass on to the rest of his family when he died. Whatever, according to Rootes long-time PR man, John Bullock, Lord Rootes was still not happy with the deal when it was signed. Talking to a trusted colleague, he reputedly commented that:

> I just hope that we have done the right thing, but I feel we may live to regret the involvement with Chrysler. I wish we could do something about it, but I suppose you are right, and there is nothing we can do now.

For Chrysler, if not for Rootes and its employees, this was really a 'dream deal'. Chrysler's first move into Europe had been when it took a 35 per cent stake in Simca (of France) in 1957, this having been raised to a controlling interest of 63 per cent in 1963. In addition, Chrysler also had a long-established truck assembly plant at Kew, in south-west London.

Lord Rootes, having speedily become disillusioned with the way Chrysler did business, and with the way the American company rapidly began to question every decision Rootes took thereafter, soon withdrew from the scene, retiring to his much-loved country home of Ramsbury Manor in Wiltshire (which, coincidentally, is very close to where this book has been published).

Once Lord Rootes had died, in December 1964, his position as chairman was taken by Sir Reginald Rootes, but a full takeover bid from Chrysler was always expected, this duly following at the beginning of 1967. Following the sale of the Dodge truck subsidiary to Rootes in 1965, Chrysler's stake had already risen to 45 per cent voting and 62 per cent non-voting shares.

After a great deal of predictable bluster in the House of Commons about control of Rootes passing out of Britain, to the USA,

Chrysler's further investment of £20 million was enough to give them majority control. Sir Reginald Rootes died, and although the second Lord Rootes (Geoffrey Rootes, Billy's son) took his place, this was never a position of power.

At the same time a new managing director was appointed, this being Gilbert Hunt, who joined Rootes from Massey Ferguson. Hunt took up his position in mid-1967, and we now know that one of his first major decisions was to kill off the Alpine.

Index